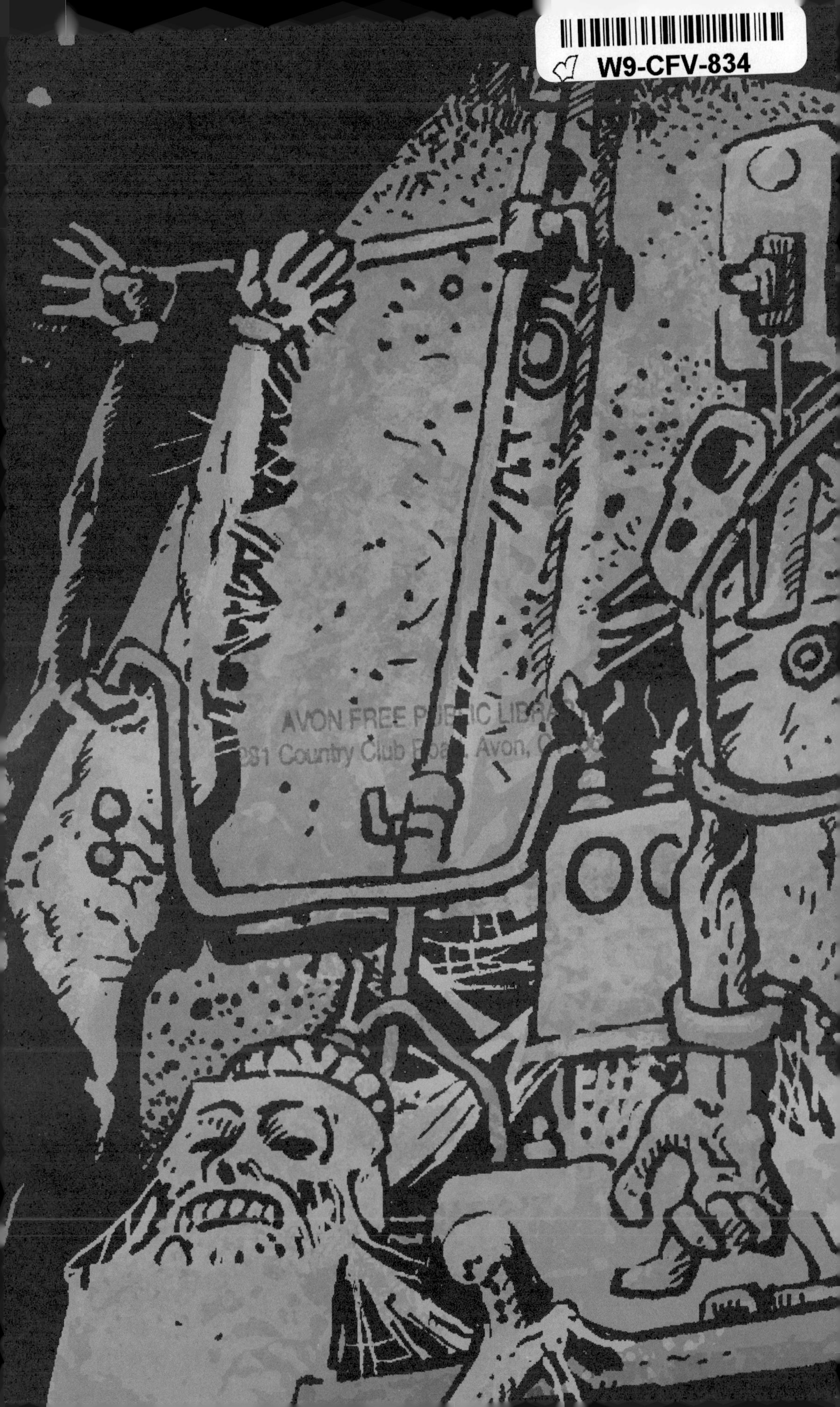

HOUSE *of the* LIVING DEAD

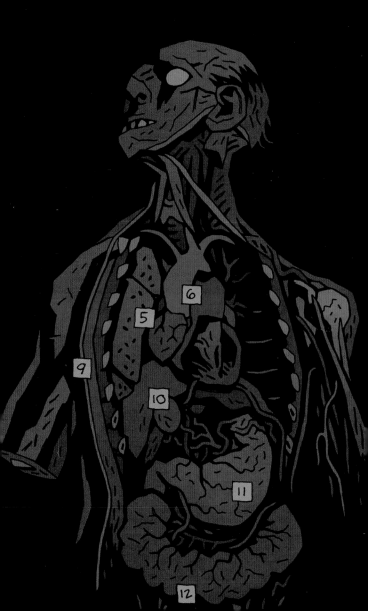

HELLBOY

HOUSE *of the* LIVING DEAD

Story by
MIKE MIGNOLA

Art by
RICHARD CORBEN

Colored by
DAVE STEWART

Lettered by
CLEM ROBINS

Editor
SCOTT ALLIE

Assistant Editor
DANIEL CHABON

Hellboy logo designed by
KEVIN NOWLAN

Collection designed by
MIKE MIGNOLA & CARY GRAZZINI

Publisher
MIKE RICHARDSON

DARK HORSE BOOKS®

Published by
Dark Horse Books
A division of Dark Horse Comics, Inc.
10956 SE Main St.
Milwaukie, OR 97222

First Edition
November 2011
ISBN 978-1-59582-757-9

1 3 5 7 9 10 8 6 4 2

Printed at 1010 Printing International, Ltd., Guangdong Province, China

For Boris Karloff (the mad scientist), Glenn Strange (the monster), John Carradine (the skinny Dracula), and Lon Chaney Jr. (the always-sad Wolf Man). This book is an affectionate nod to Universal's sort-of terrible (but if you grew up with them, they will always be great) *House of Dracula* and *House of Frankenstein.*

Also, I guess, for all those Mexican-wrestler-vs.-monster movies (such as *Santo vs. Las Mujeres Vampiro*)—I've never actually seen any of them, but I sure love the *idea* of them.

MIKE MIGNOLA

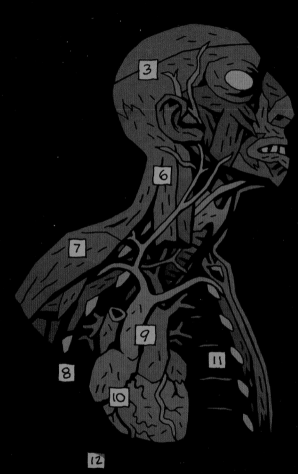

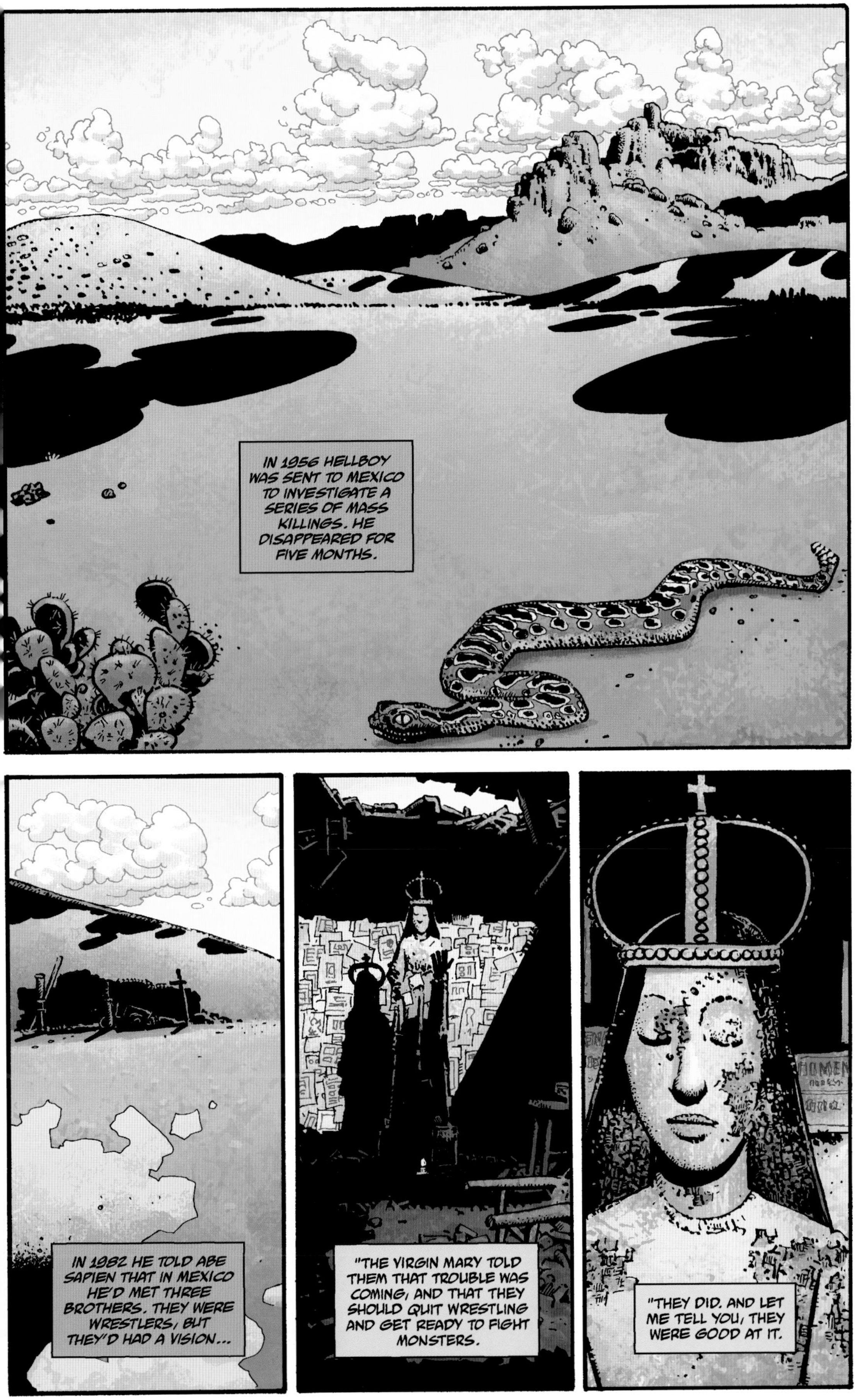
IN 1956 HELLBOY WAS SENT TO MEXICO TO INVESTIGATE A SERIES OF MASS KILLINGS. HE DISAPPEARED FOR FIVE MONTHS.
IN 1982 HE TOLD ABE SAPIEN THAT IN MEXICO HE'D MET THREE BROTHERS. THEY WERE WRESTLERS, BUT THEY'D HAD A VISION...
"THE VIRGIN MARY TOLD THEM THAT TROUBLE WAS COMING, AND THAT THEY SHOULD QUIT WRESTLING AND GET READY TO FIGHT MONSTERS.
"THEY DID. AND LET ME TELL YOU, THEY WERE GOOD AT IT.

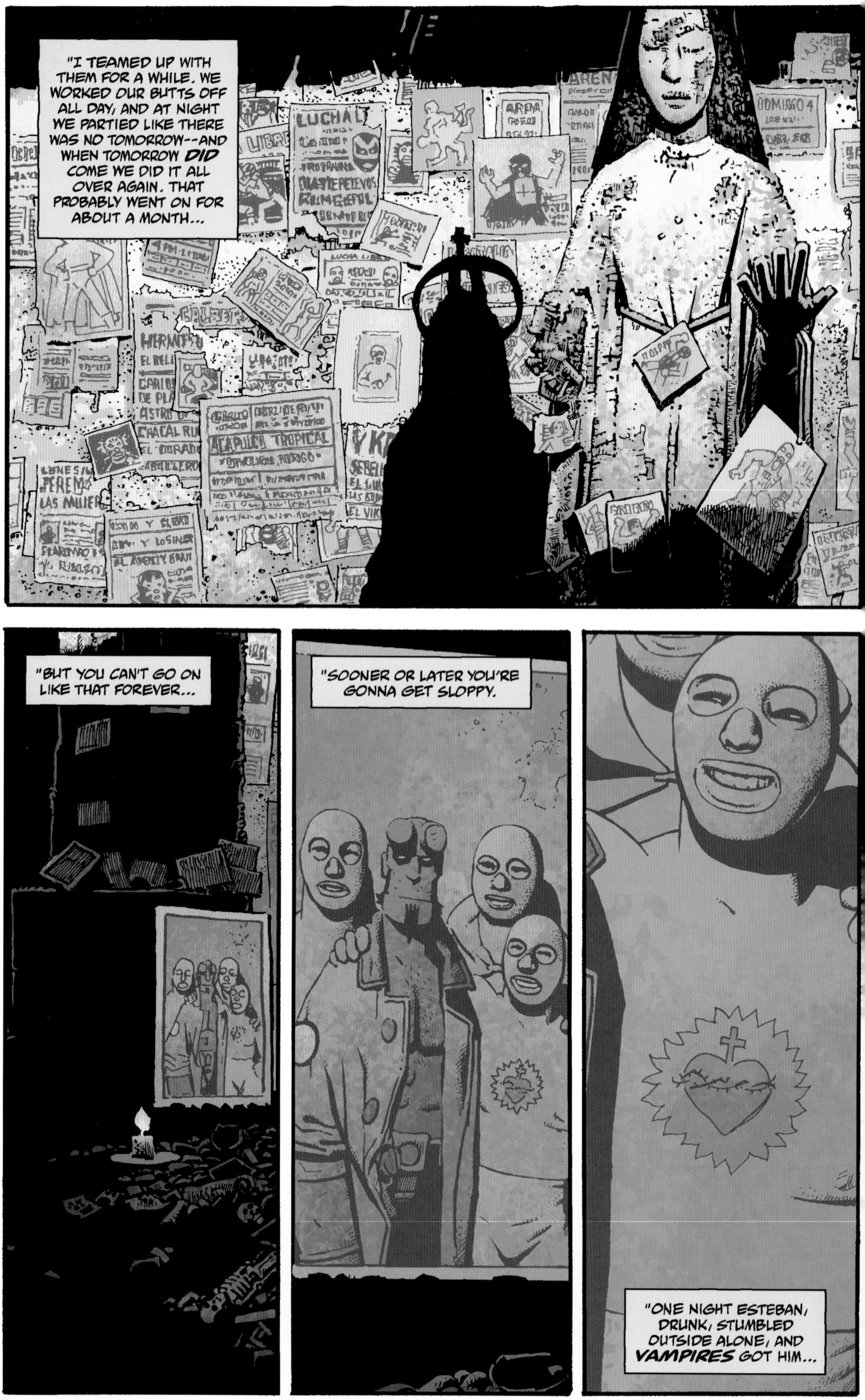
"I TEAMED UP WITH THEM FOR A WHILE. WE WORKED OUR BUTTS OFF ALL DAY, AND AT NIGHT WE PARTIED LIKE THERE WAS NO TOMORROW--AND WHEN TOMORROW DID COME WE DID IT ALL OVER AGAIN. THAT PROBABLY WENT ON FOR ABOUT A MONTH...
"BUT YOU CAN'T GO ON LIKE THAT FOREVER...
"SOONER OR LATER YOU'RE GONNA GET SLOPPY.
"ONE NIGHT ESTEBAN, DRUNK, STUMBLED OUTSIDE ALONE, AND VAMPIRES GOT HIM...

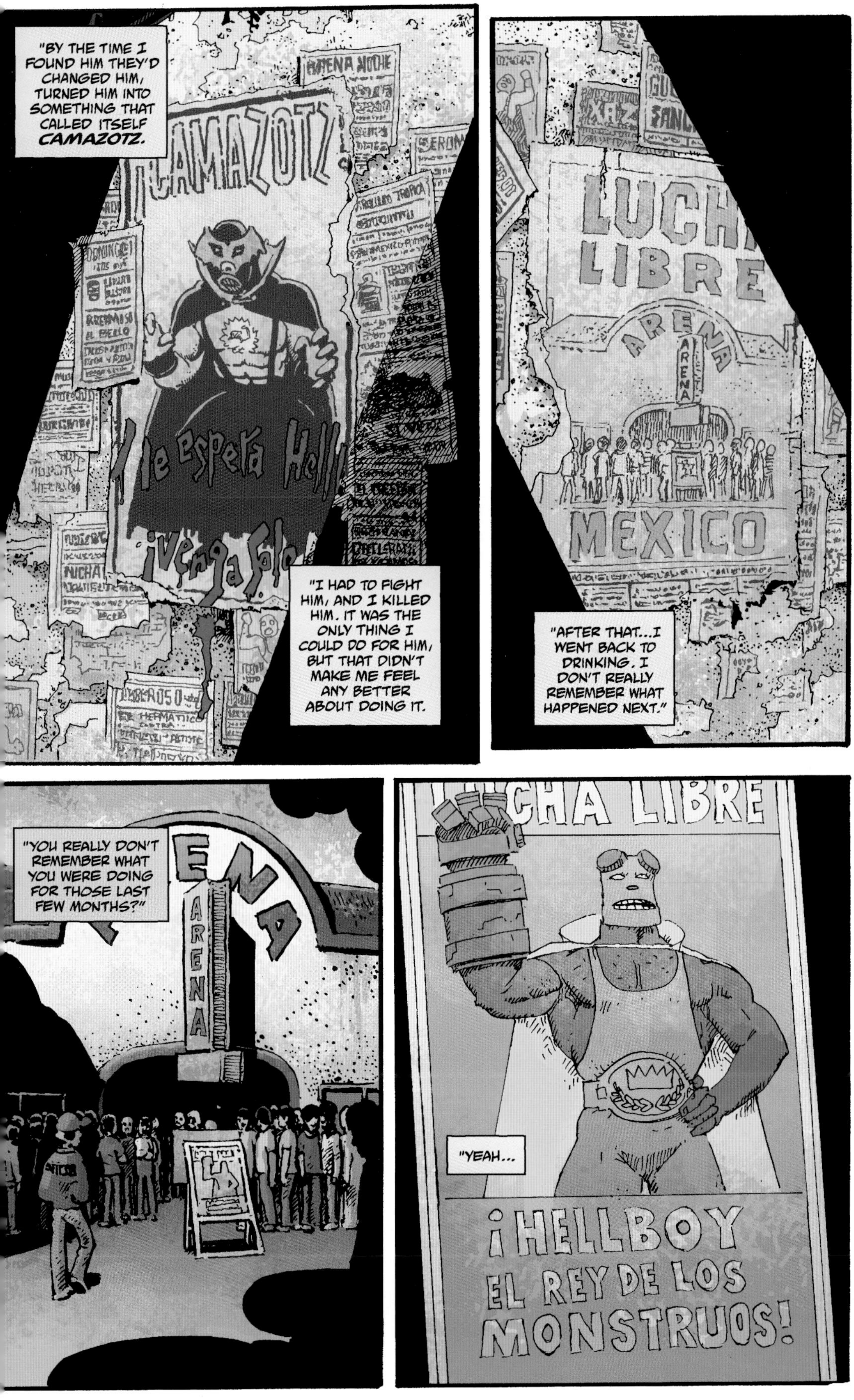
"BY THE TIME I FOUND HIM THEY'D CHANGED HIM, TURNED HIM INTO SOMETHING THAT CALLED ITSELF **CAMAZOTZ.**
CAMAZOTZ
"I HAD TO FIGHT HIM, AND I KILLED HIM. IT WAS THE ONLY THING I COULD DO FOR HIM, BUT THAT DIDN'T MAKE ME FEEL ANY BETTER ABOUT DOING IT.
LIBRE
ARENA
MEXICO
"AFTER THAT...I WENT BACK TO DRINKING. I DON'T REALLY REMEMBER WHAT HAPPENED NEXT."
"YOU REALLY DON'T REMEMBER WHAT YOU WERE DOING FOR THOSE LAST FEW MONTHS?"
ARENA
"YEAH...
¡HELLBOY EL REY DE LOS MONSTRUOS!

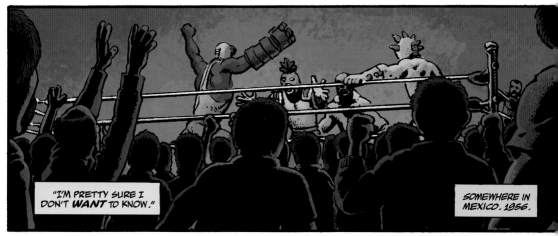

"I'M PRETTY SURE I DON'T **WANT** TO KNOW."

SOMEWHERE IN MEXICO. 1956.

ERRR! UGH!

UUAH!

GAA!

HUUAH!

AHH!

OOF!

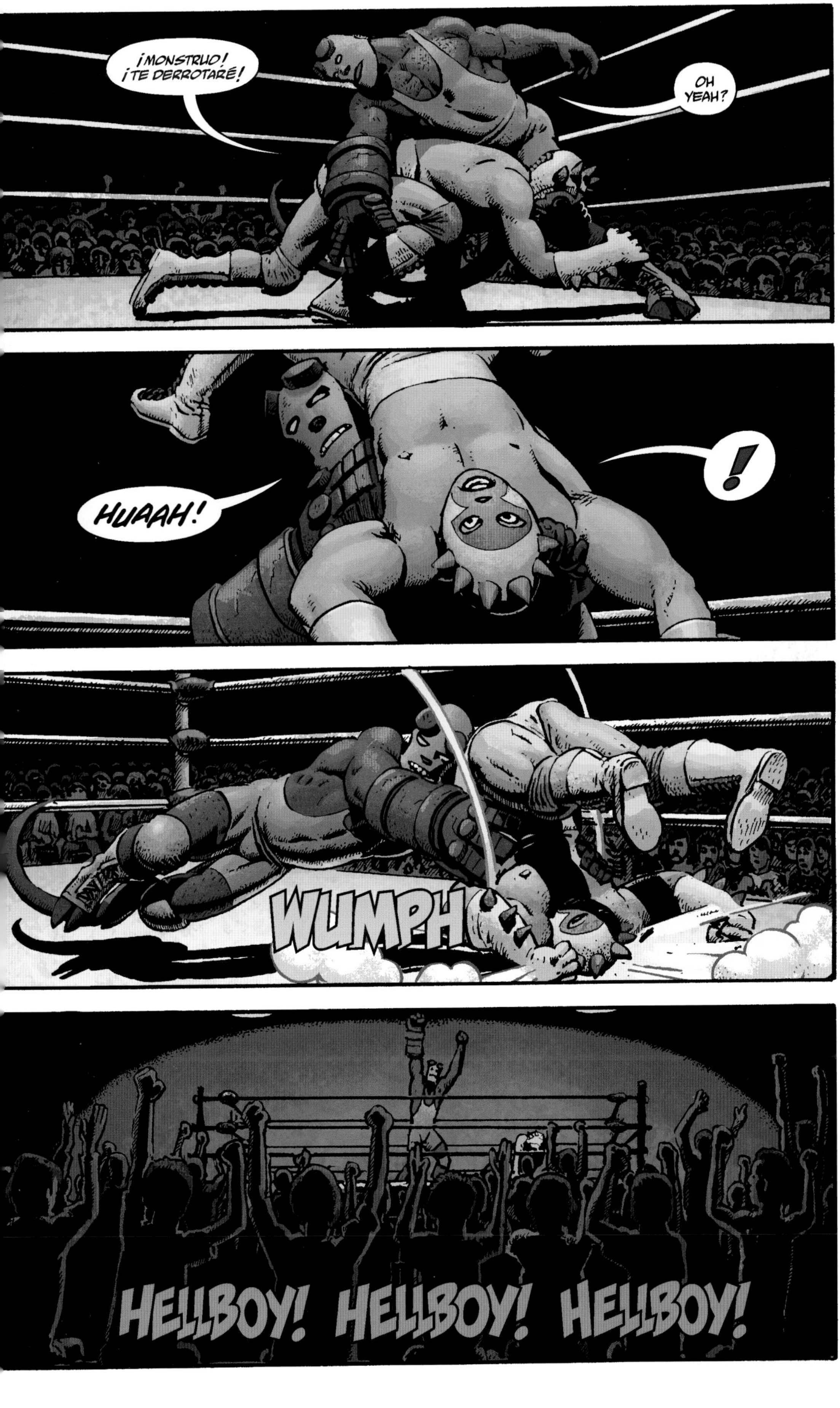
¡MONSTRUO! ¡TE DERROTARÉ!
OH YEAH?
HUAAH!
!
WUMPH
HELLBOY! HELLBOY! HELLBOY!

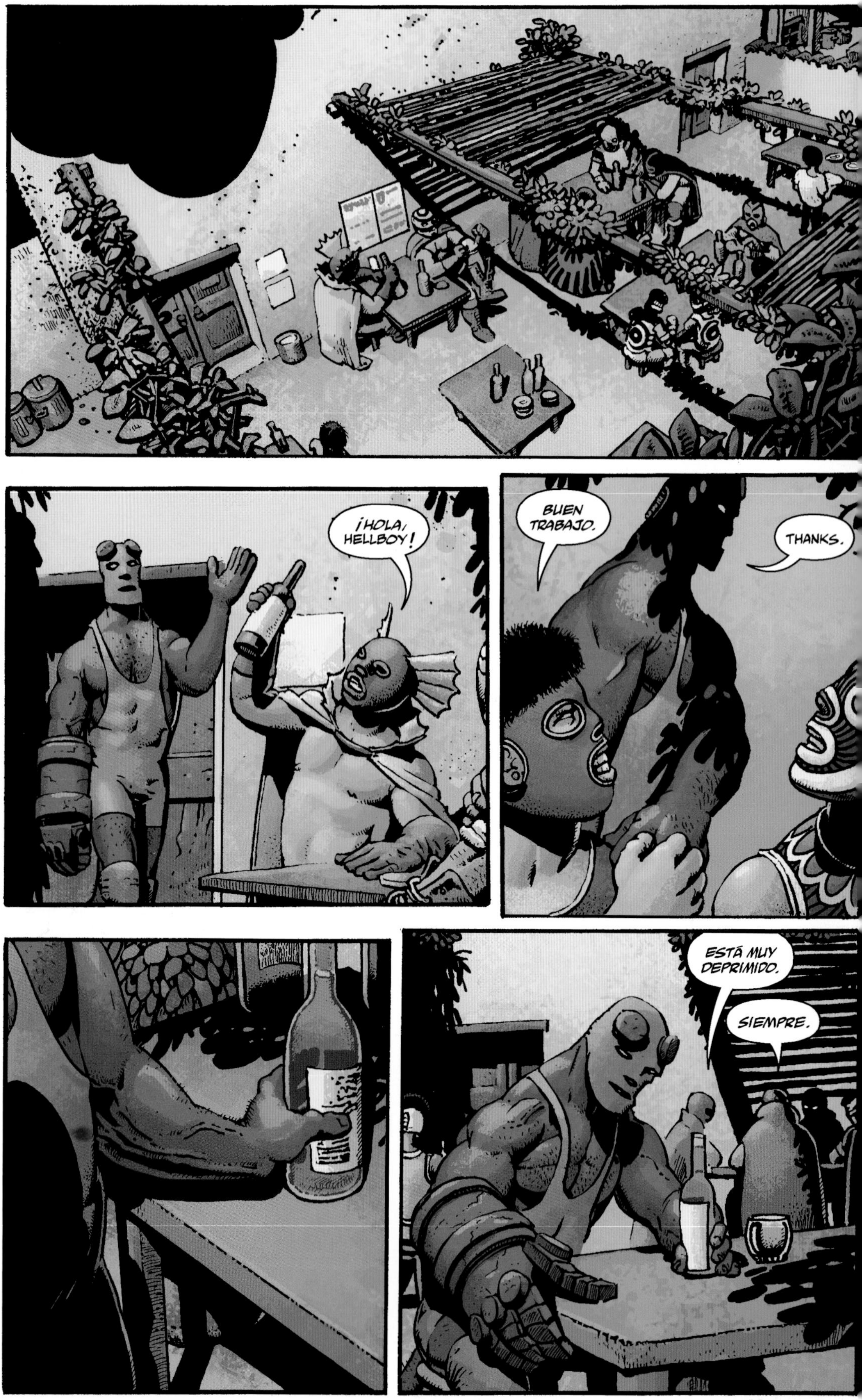
¡HOLA, HELLBOY!
BUEN TRABAJO.
THANKS.
ESTÁ MUY DEPRIMIDO.
SIEMPRE.

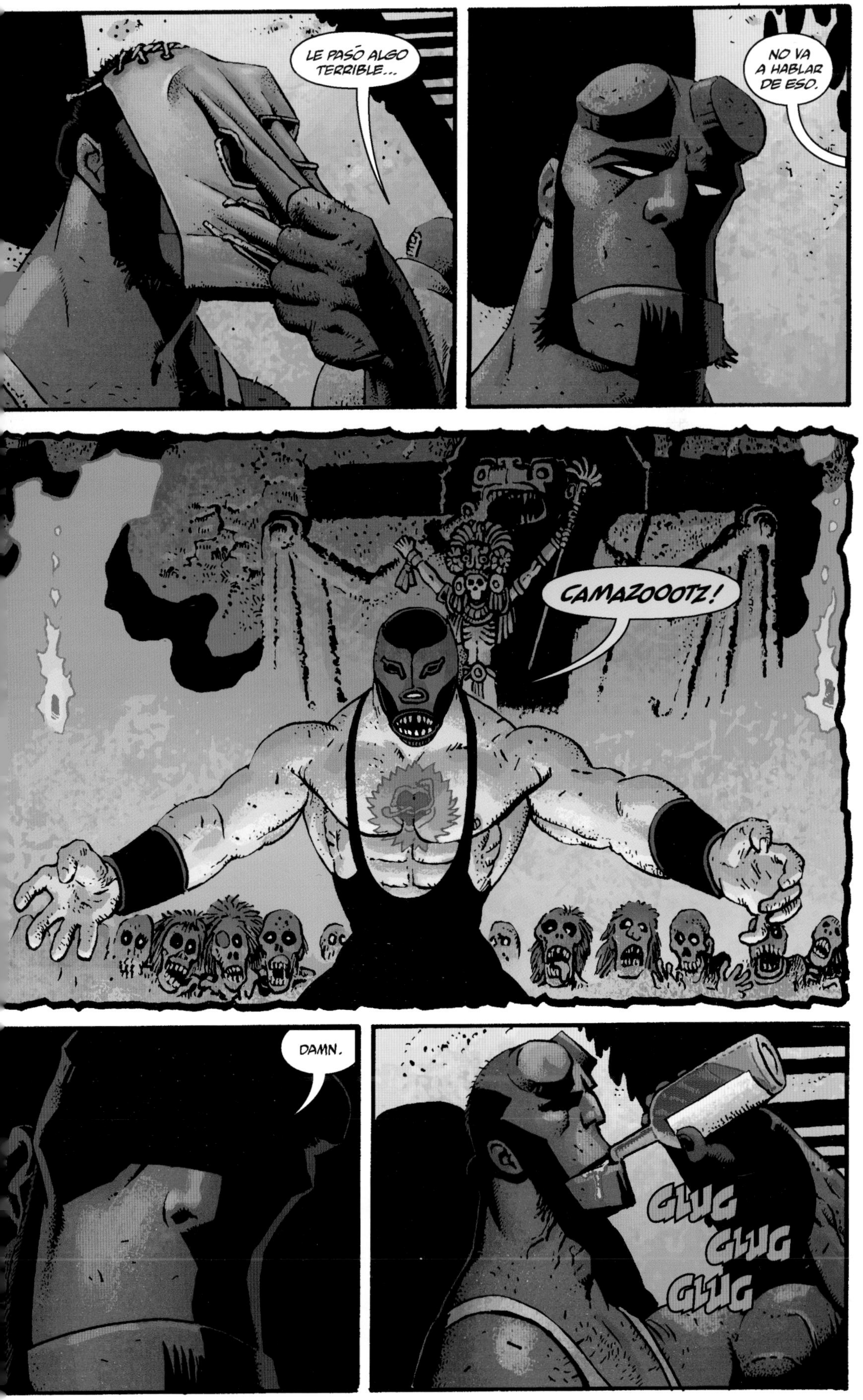
LE PASÓ ALGO TERRIBLE...
NO VA A HABLAR DE ESO.
CAMAZOOOTZ!
DAMN.
GLUG
GLUG
GLUG

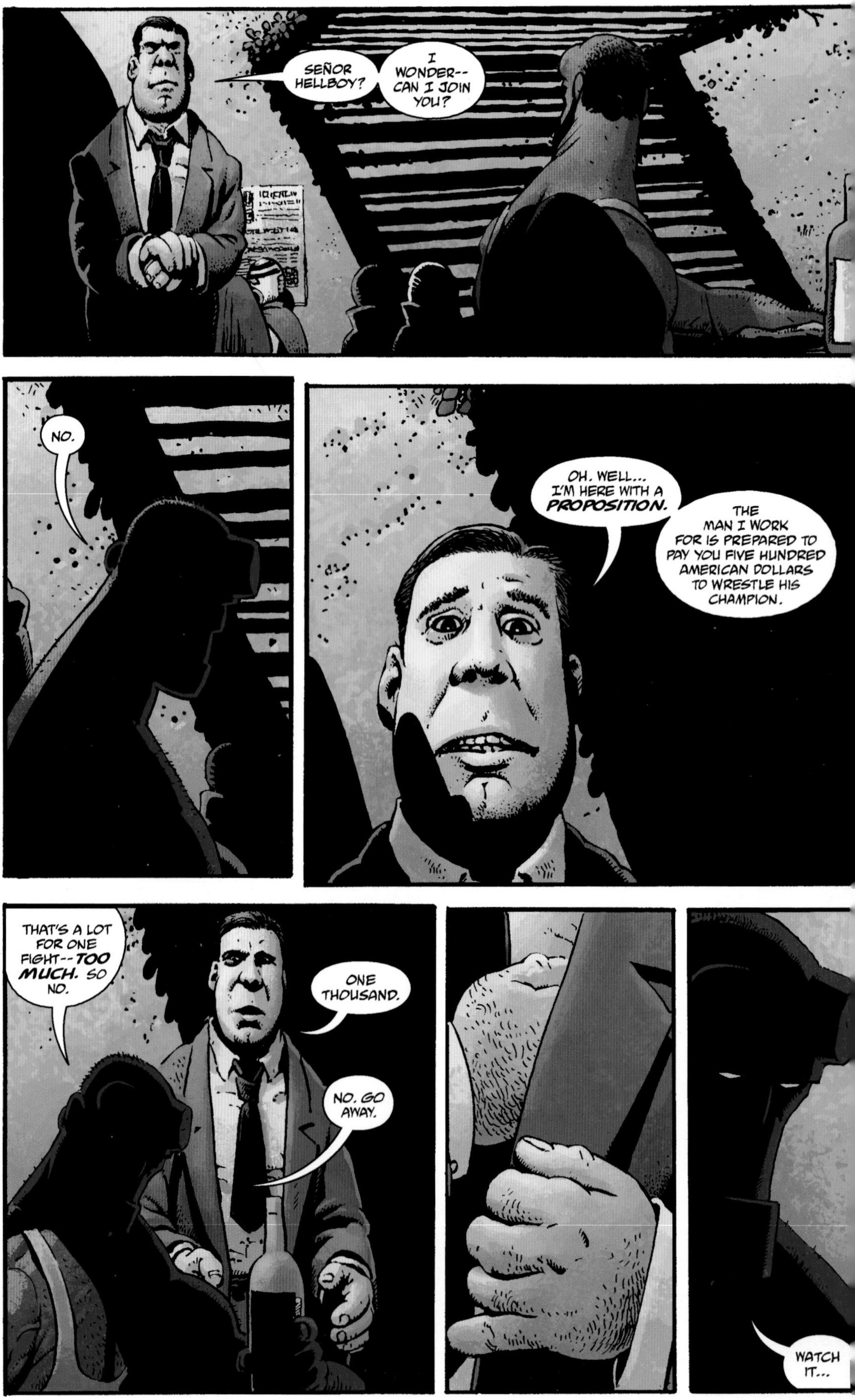
SEÑOR HELLBOY?
I WONDER-- CAN I JOIN YOU?
NO.
OH. WELL... I'M HERE WITH A PROPOSITION.
THE MAN I WORK FOR IS PREPARED TO PAY YOU FIVE HUNDRED AMERICAN DOLLARS TO WRESTLE HIS CHAMPION.
THAT'S A LOT FOR ONE FIGHT--TOO MUCH. SO NO.
ONE THOUSAND.
NO. GO AWAY.
WATCH IT...

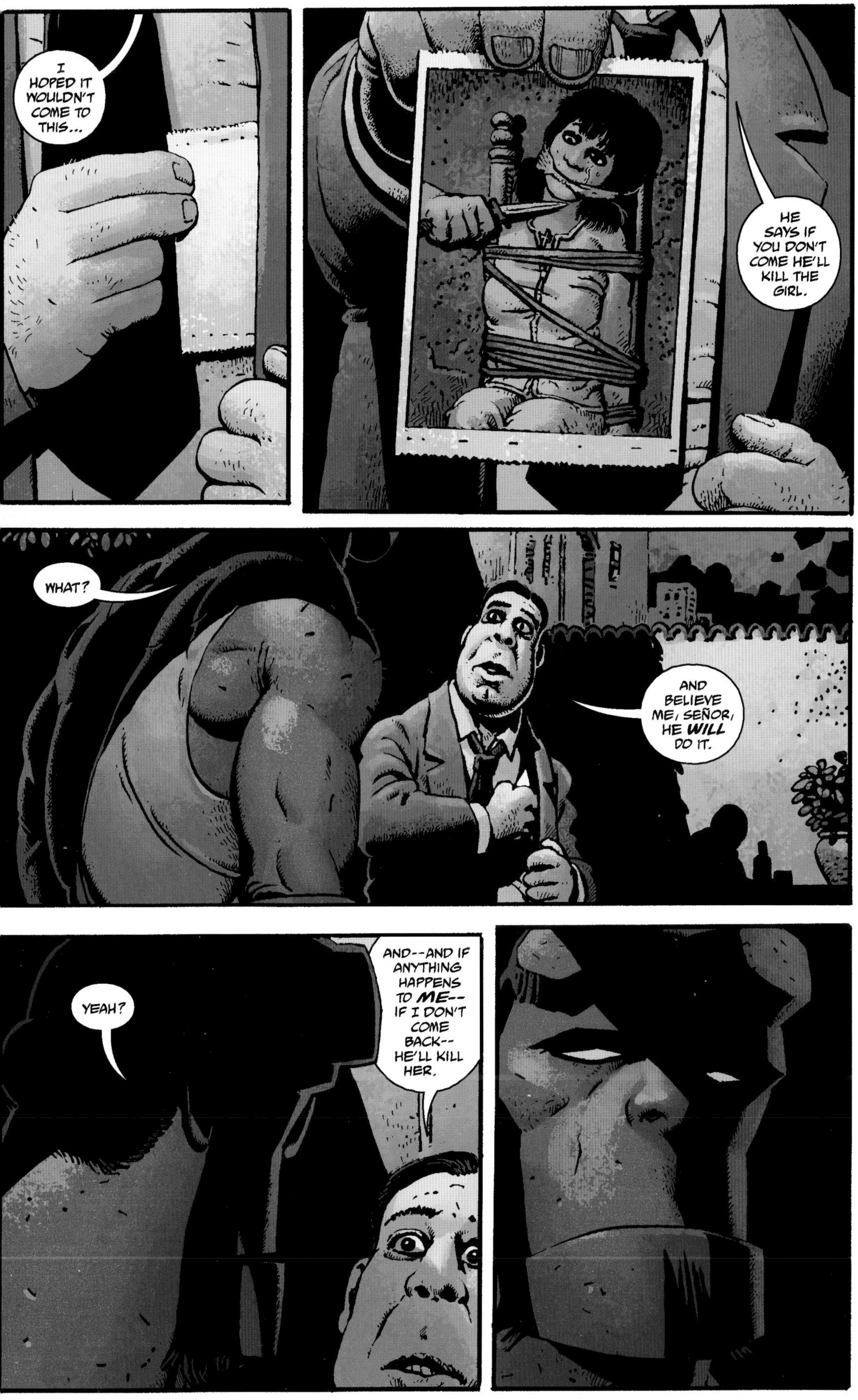
I HOPED IT WOULDN'T COME TO THIS...
HE SAYS IF YOU DON'T COME HE'LL KILL THE GIRL.
WHAT?
AND BELIEVE ME, SEÑOR, HE WILL DO IT.
YEAH?
AND--AND IF ANYTHING HAPPENS TO ME-- IF I DON'T COME BACK-- HE'LL KILL HER.

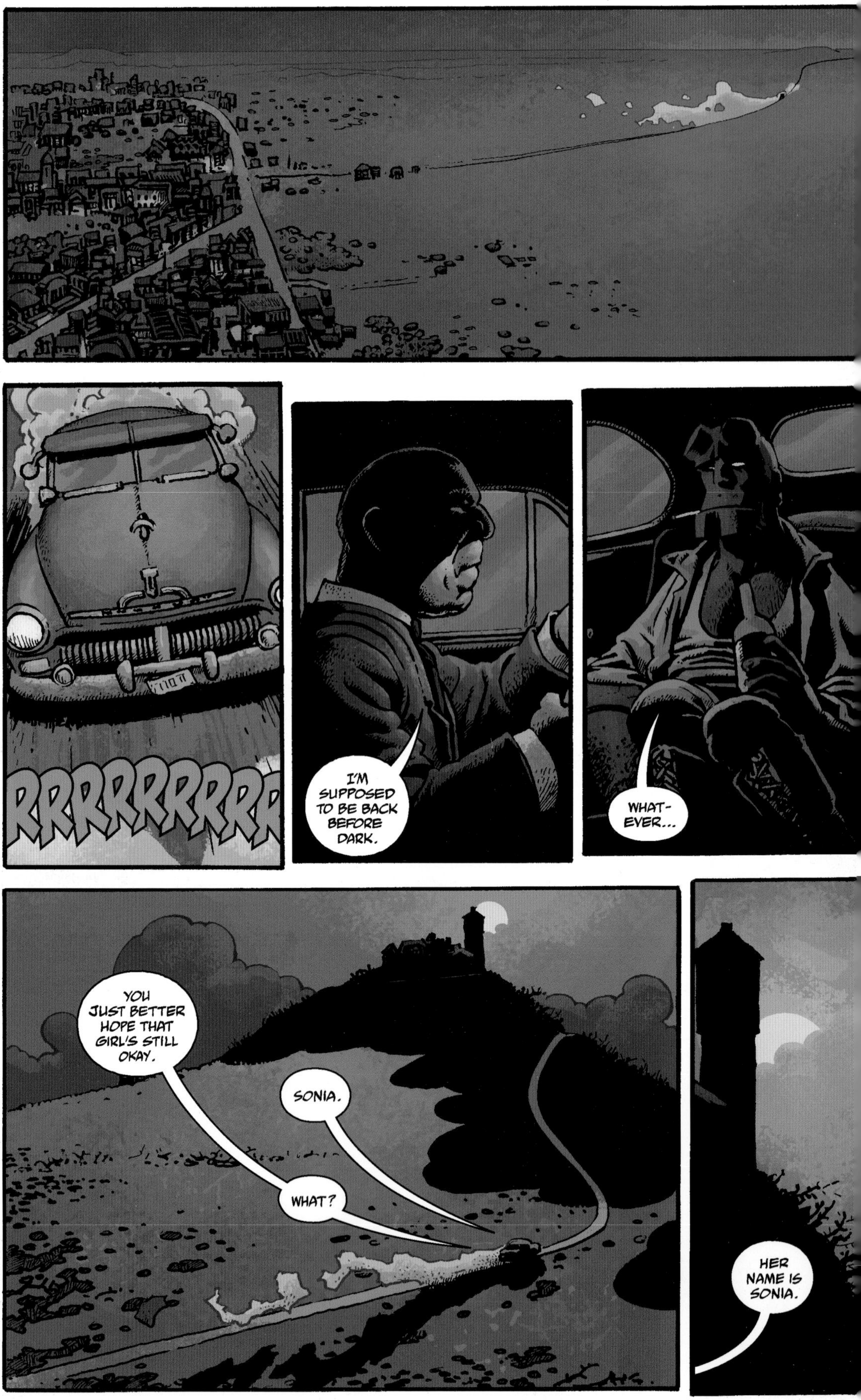
RRRRRRRRRR
I'M SUPPOSED TO BE BACK BEFORE DARK.
WHAT-EVER...
YOU JUST BETTER HOPE THAT GIRL'S STILL OKAY.
SONIA.
WHAT?
HER NAME IS SONIA.

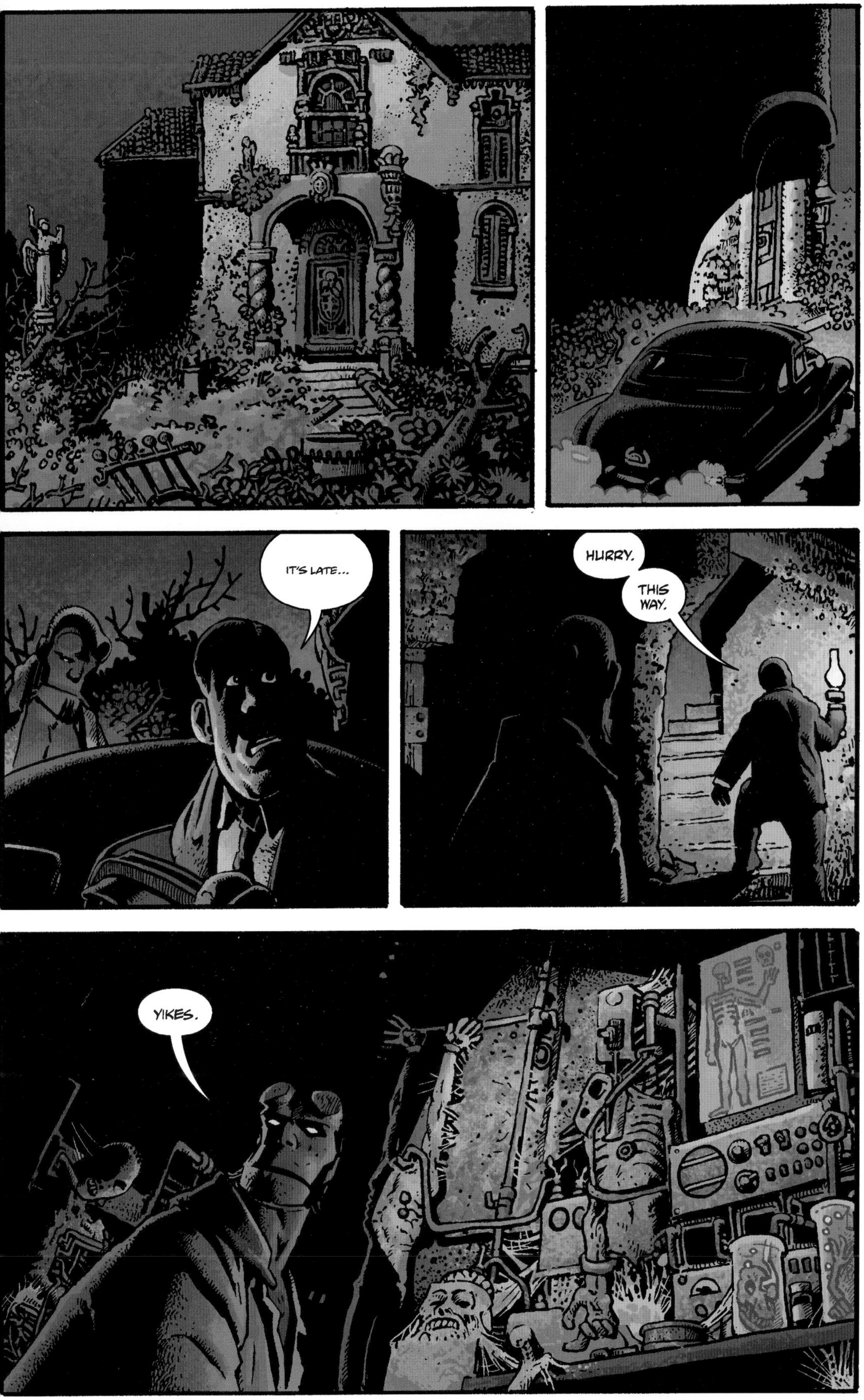
IT'S LATE...
HURRY.
THIS WAY.
YIKES.

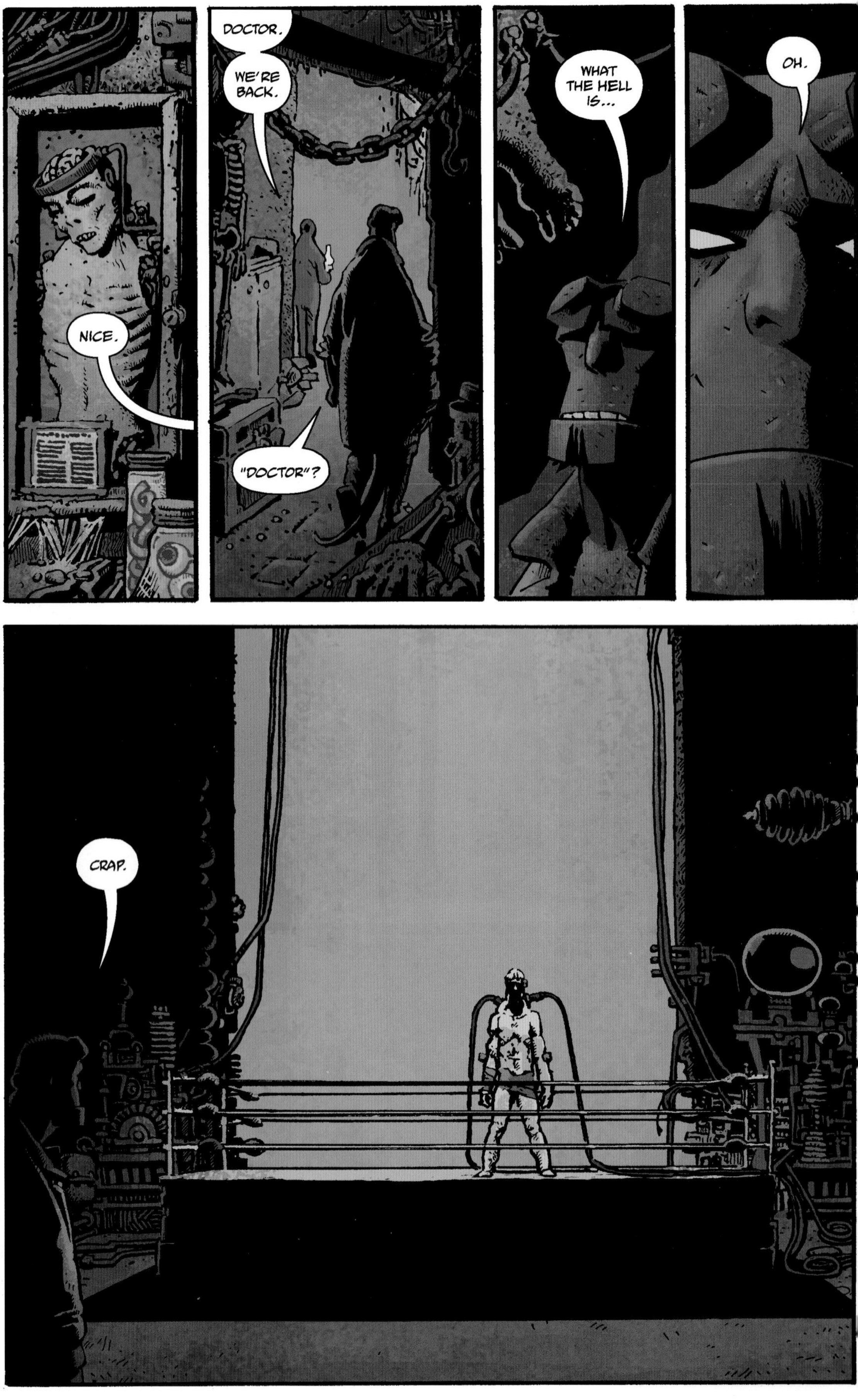
NICE.
DOCTOR.
WE'RE BACK.
"DOCTOR"?
WHAT THE HELL IS...
OH.
CRAP.

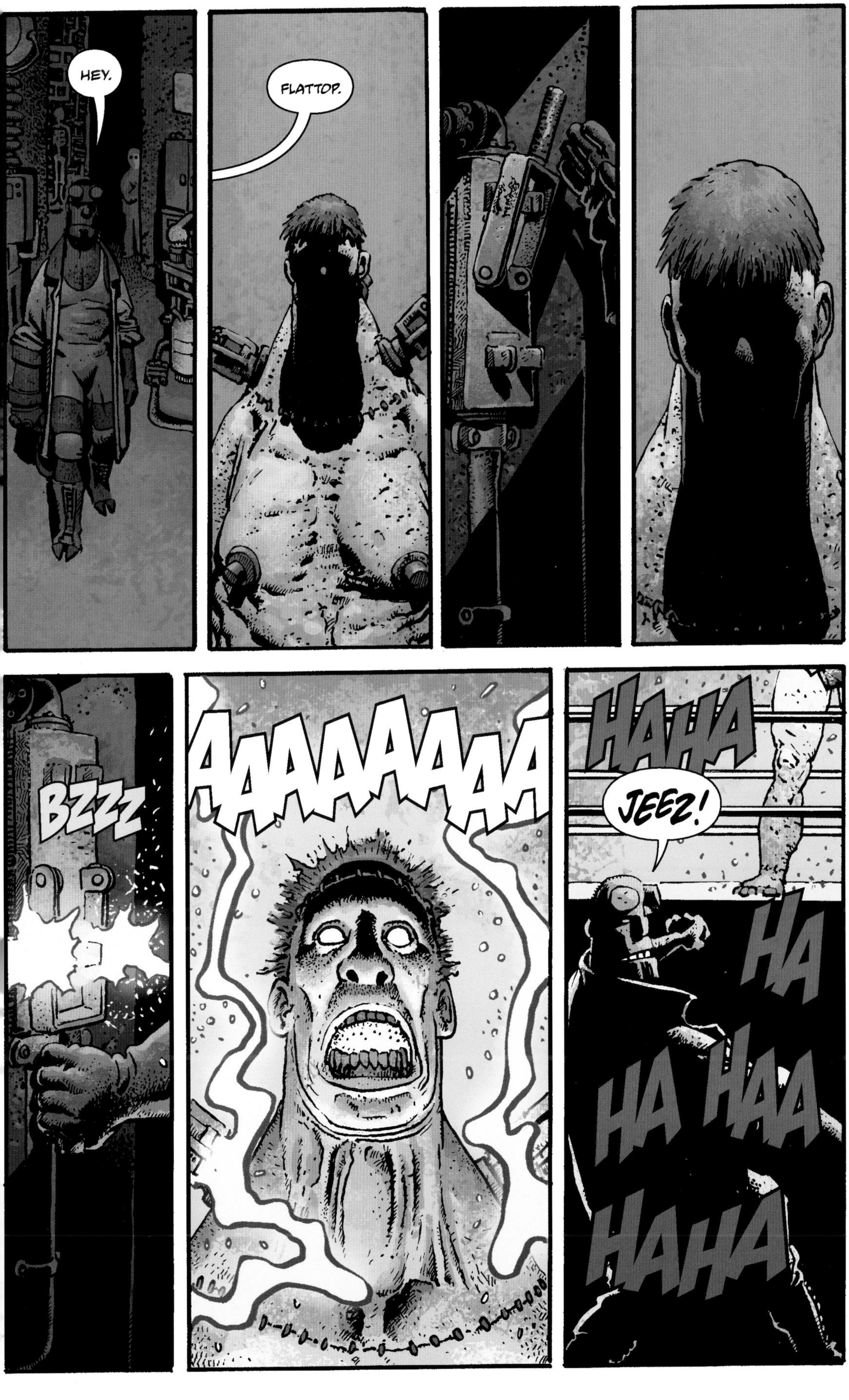
HEY.
FLATTOP.
BZZZ
AAAAAAAA
HAHA
JEEZ!
HA
HA HAA
HAHA

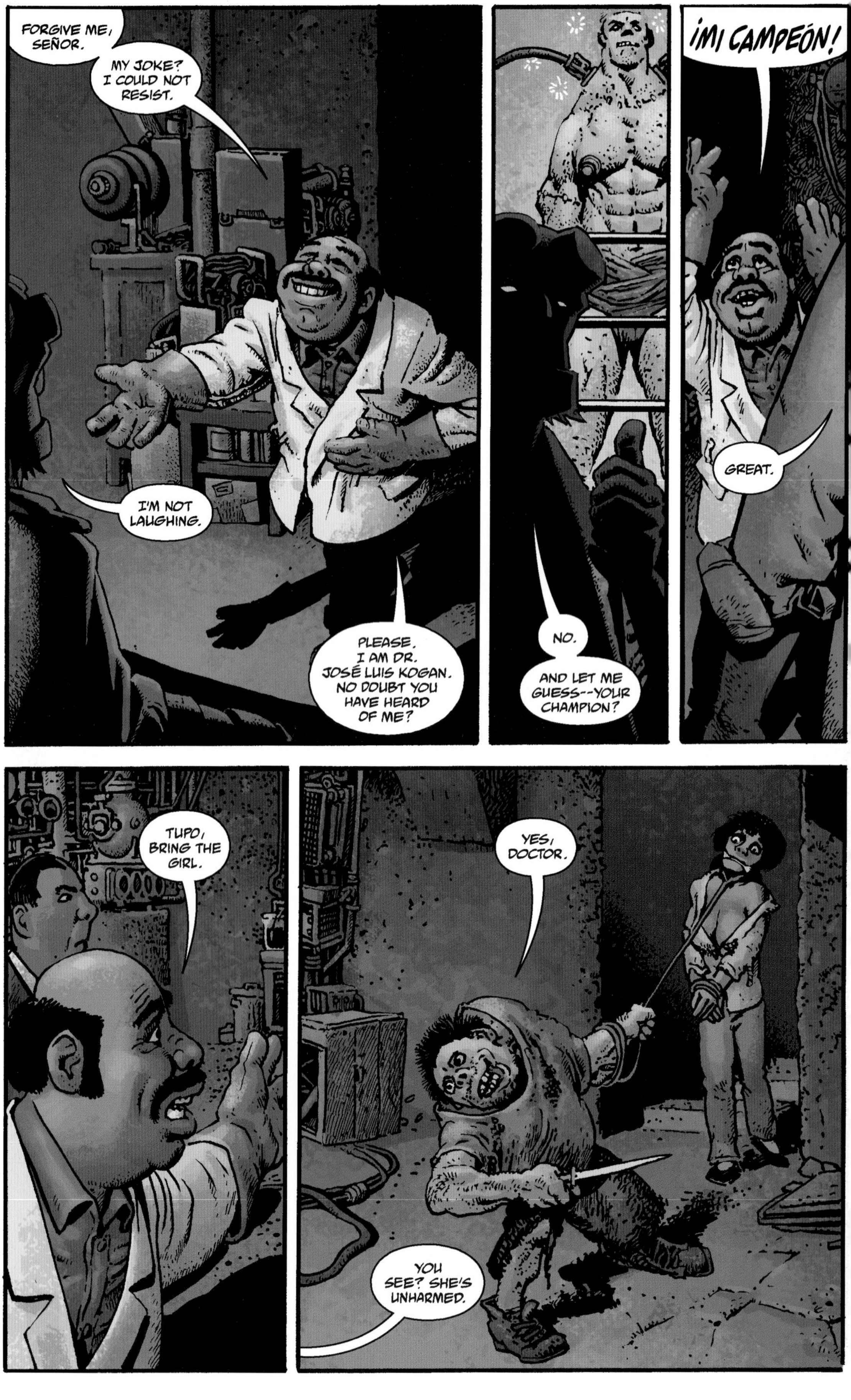
FORGIVE ME, SEÑOR.
MY JOKE? I COULD NOT RESIST.
I'M NOT LAUGHING.
PLEASE. I AM DR. JOSÉ LUIS KOGAN. NO DOUBT YOU HAVE HEARD OF ME?
NO.
AND LET ME GUESS--YOUR CHAMPION?
¡MI CAMPEÓN!
GREAT.
TUPO, BRING THE GIRL.
YES, DOCTOR.
YOU SEE? SHE'S UNHARMED.

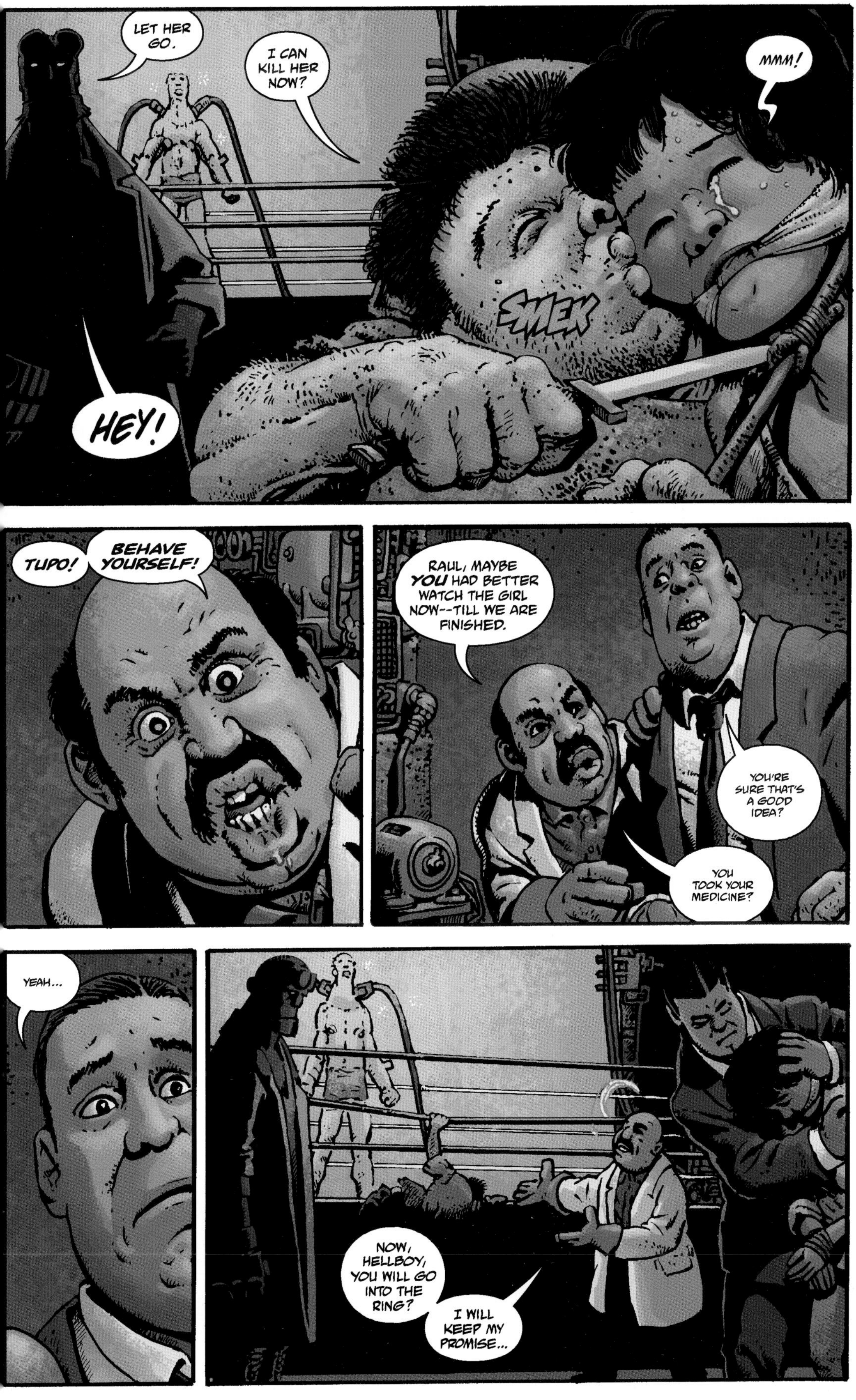
LET HER GO.
I CAN KILL HER NOW?
MMM!
SMEK
HEY!
TUPO!
BEHAVE YOURSELF!
RAUL, MAYBE YOU HAD BETTER WATCH THE GIRL NOW--TILL WE ARE FINISHED.
YOU'RE SURE THAT'S A GOOD IDEA?
YOU TOOK YOUR MEDICINE?
YEAH...
NOW, HELLBOY, YOU WILL GO INTO THE RING?
I WILL KEEP MY PROMISE...

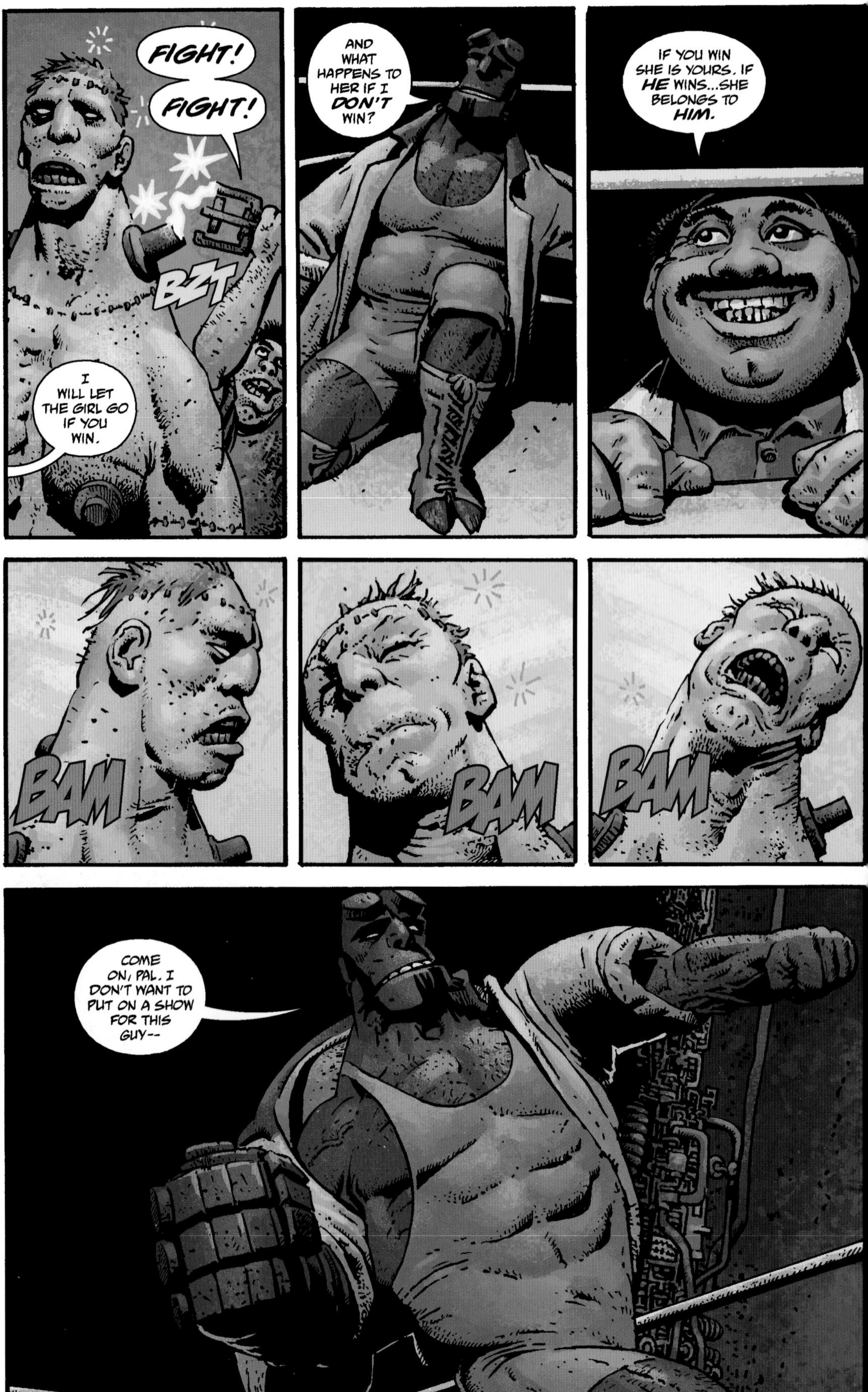
FIGHT!
FIGHT!
BZZT
I WILL LET THE GIRL GO IF YOU WIN.
AND WHAT HAPPENS TO HER IF I DON'T WIN?
IF YOU WIN SHE IS YOURS. IF HE WINS...SHE BELONGS TO HIM.
BAM
BAM
BAM
COME ON, PAL. I DON'T WANT TO PUT ON A SHOW FOR THIS GUY--

JUST FALL DOWN!
BAM
FIGHT BACK!
FIGHT!
FIIIGHT!
¡ESTÚPIDO!
FIGHT!
FIGHT!
FIGHT!
WUP

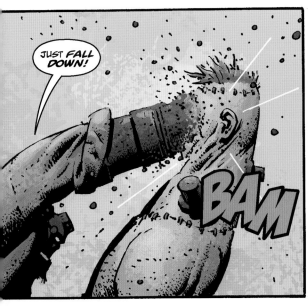

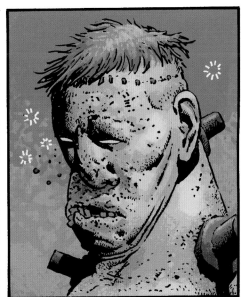

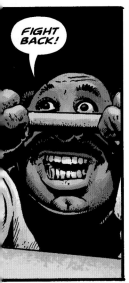

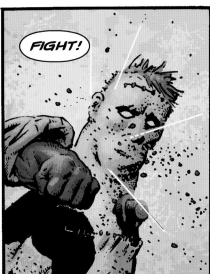

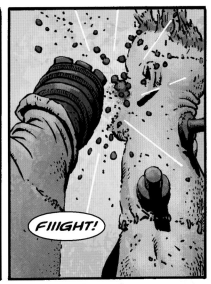

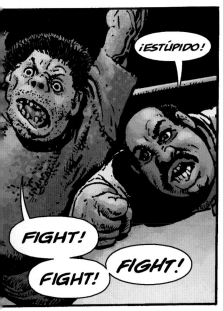

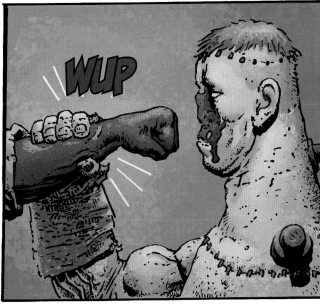

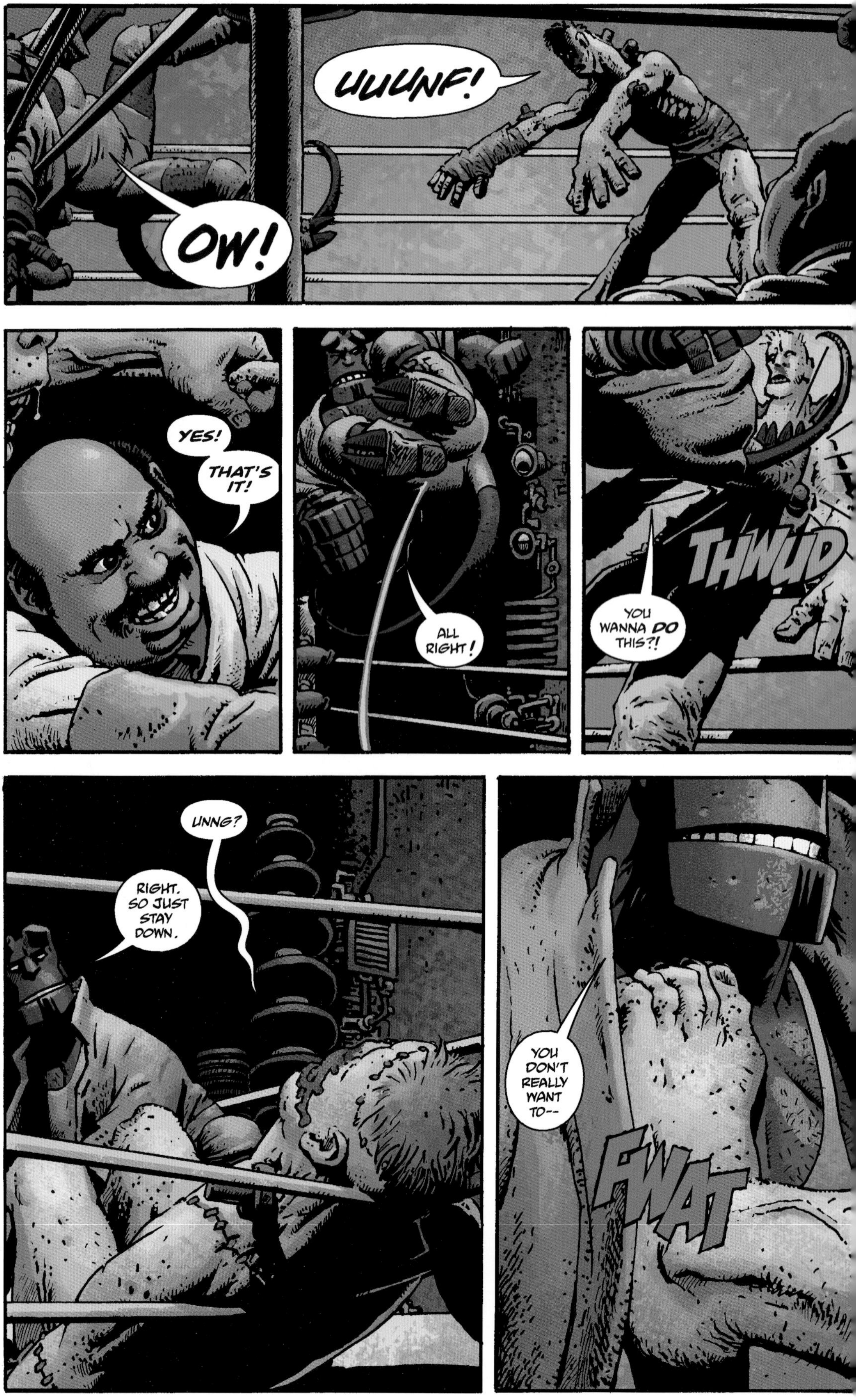
UUUNF!
OW!
YES!
THAT'S IT!
ALL RIGHT!
THWUD
YOU WANNA DO THIS?!
UNNG?
RIGHT. SO JUST STAY DOWN.
YOU DON'T REALLY WANT TO--
FWAT

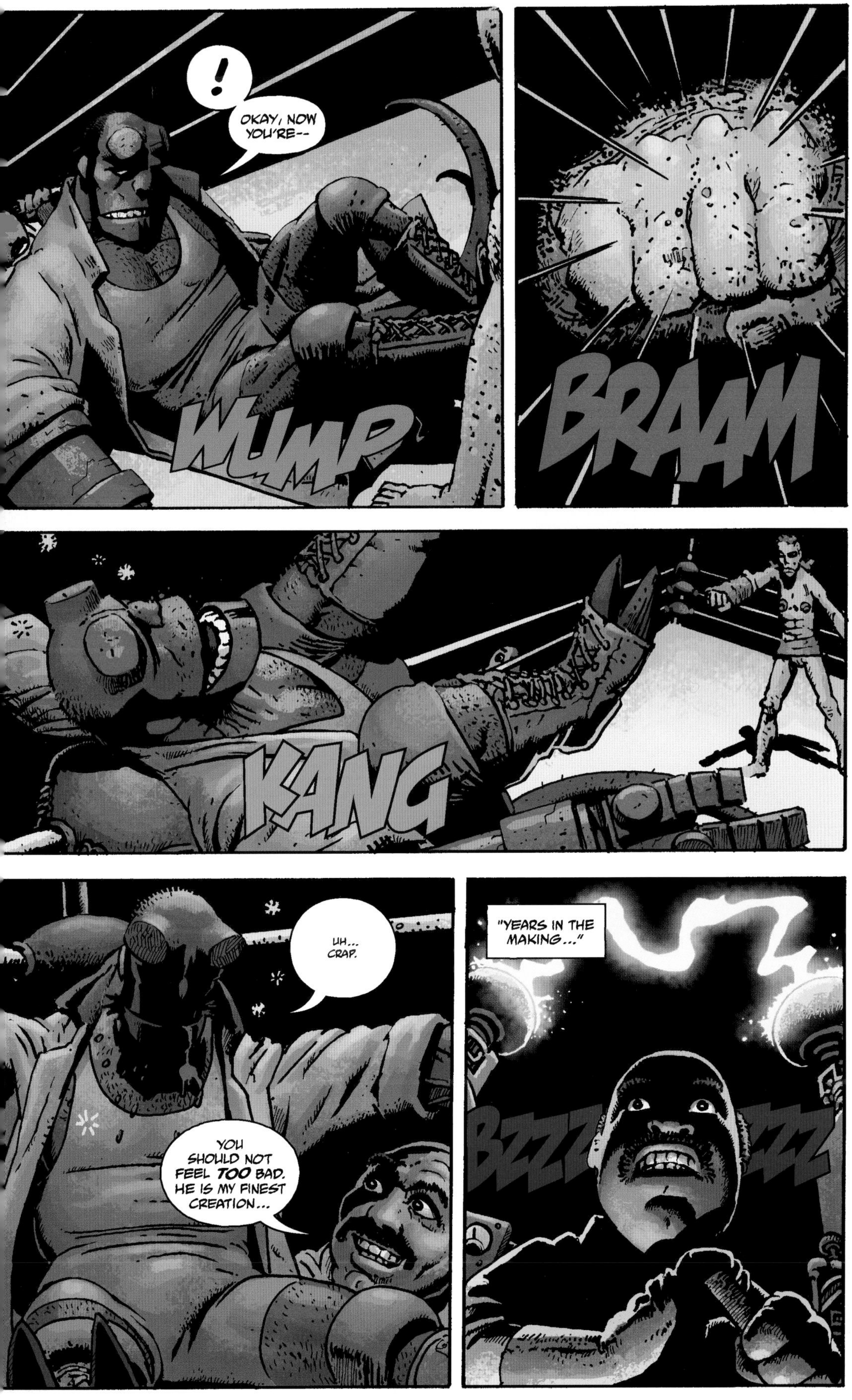
!
OKAY, NOW YOU'RE--
WUMP
BRAAM
KANG
UH... CRAP.
YOU SHOULD NOT FEEL TOO BAD. HE IS MY FINEST CREATION...
"YEARS IN THE MAKING..."
BZZZ
ZZZ

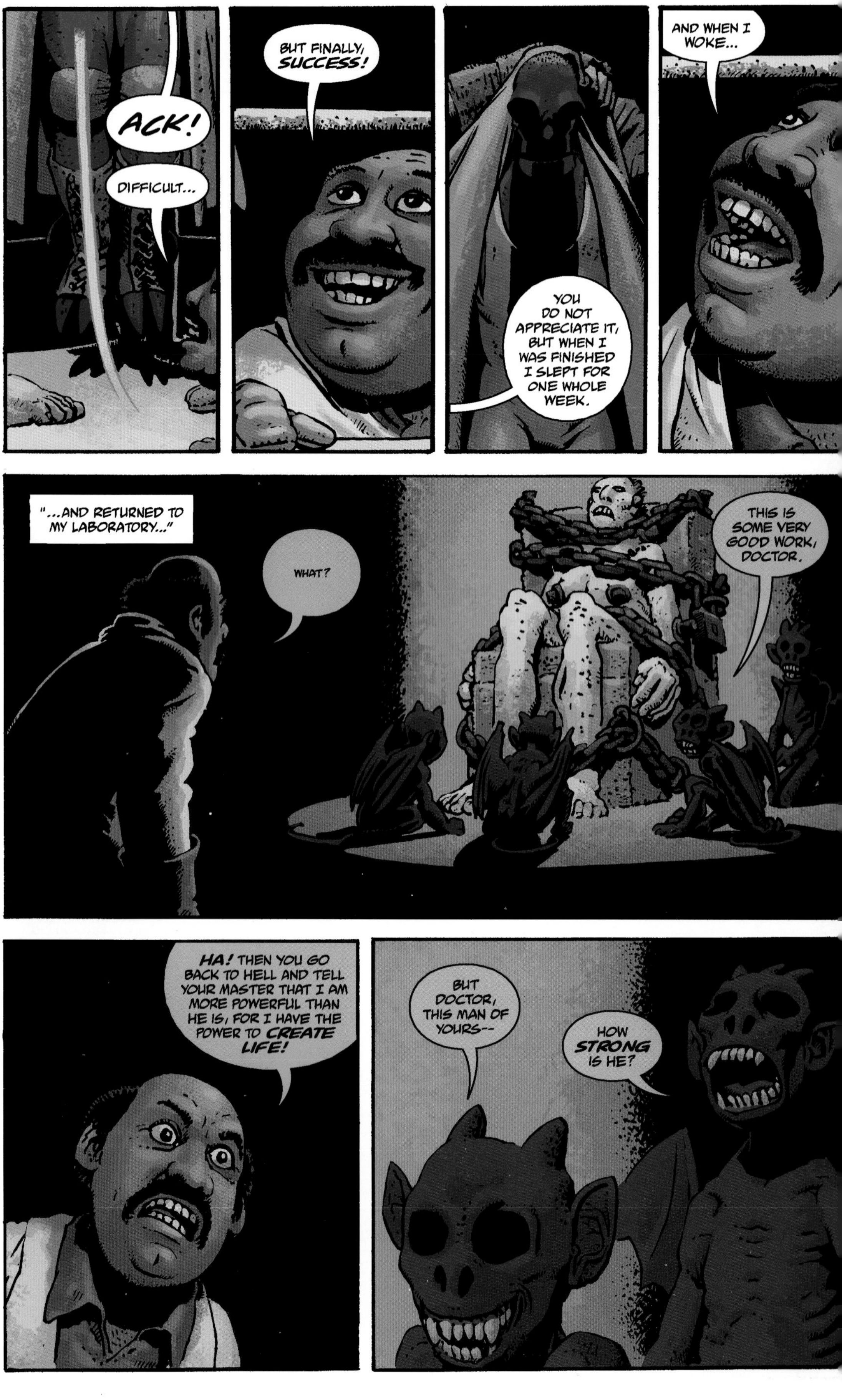
ACK!
DIFFICULT...
BUT FINALLY, SUCCESS!
YOU DO NOT APPRECIATE IT, BUT WHEN I WAS FINISHED I SLEPT FOR ONE WHOLE WEEK.
AND WHEN I WOKE...
"...AND RETURNED TO MY LABORATORY..."
WHAT?
THIS IS SOME VERY GOOD WORK, DOCTOR.
HA! THEN YOU GO BACK TO HELL AND TELL YOUR MASTER THAT I AM MORE POWERFUL THAN HE IS, FOR I HAVE THE POWER TO CREATE LIFE!
BUT DOCTOR, THIS MAN OF YOURS--
HOW STRONG IS HE?

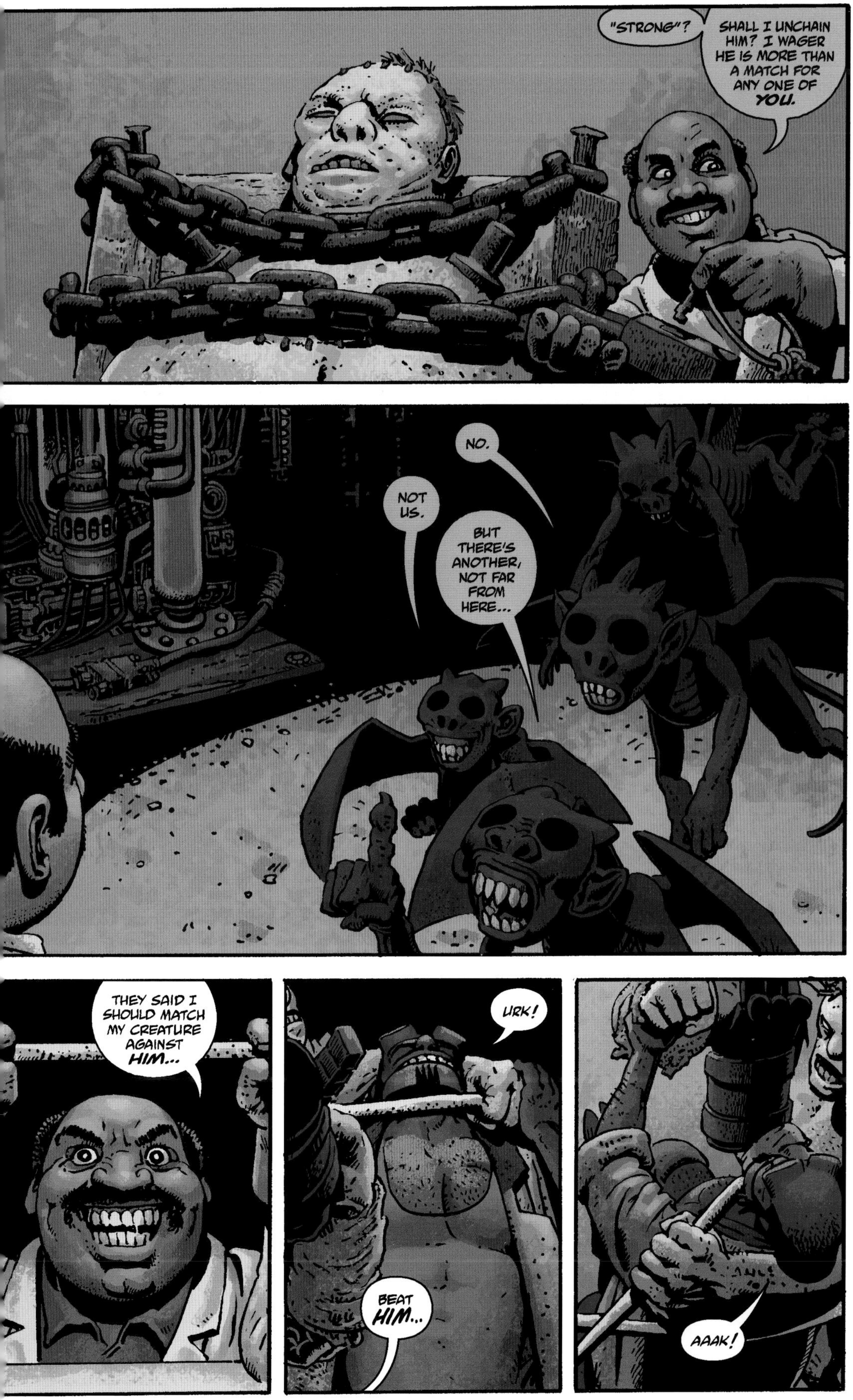
"STRONG"?
SHALL I UNCHAIN HIM? I WAGER HE IS MORE THAN A MATCH FOR ANY ONE OF YOU.
NO.
NOT US.
BUT THERE'S ANOTHER, NOT FAR FROM HERE...
THEY SAID I SHOULD MATCH MY CREATURE AGAINST HIM...
URK!
BEAT HIM...
AAAK!

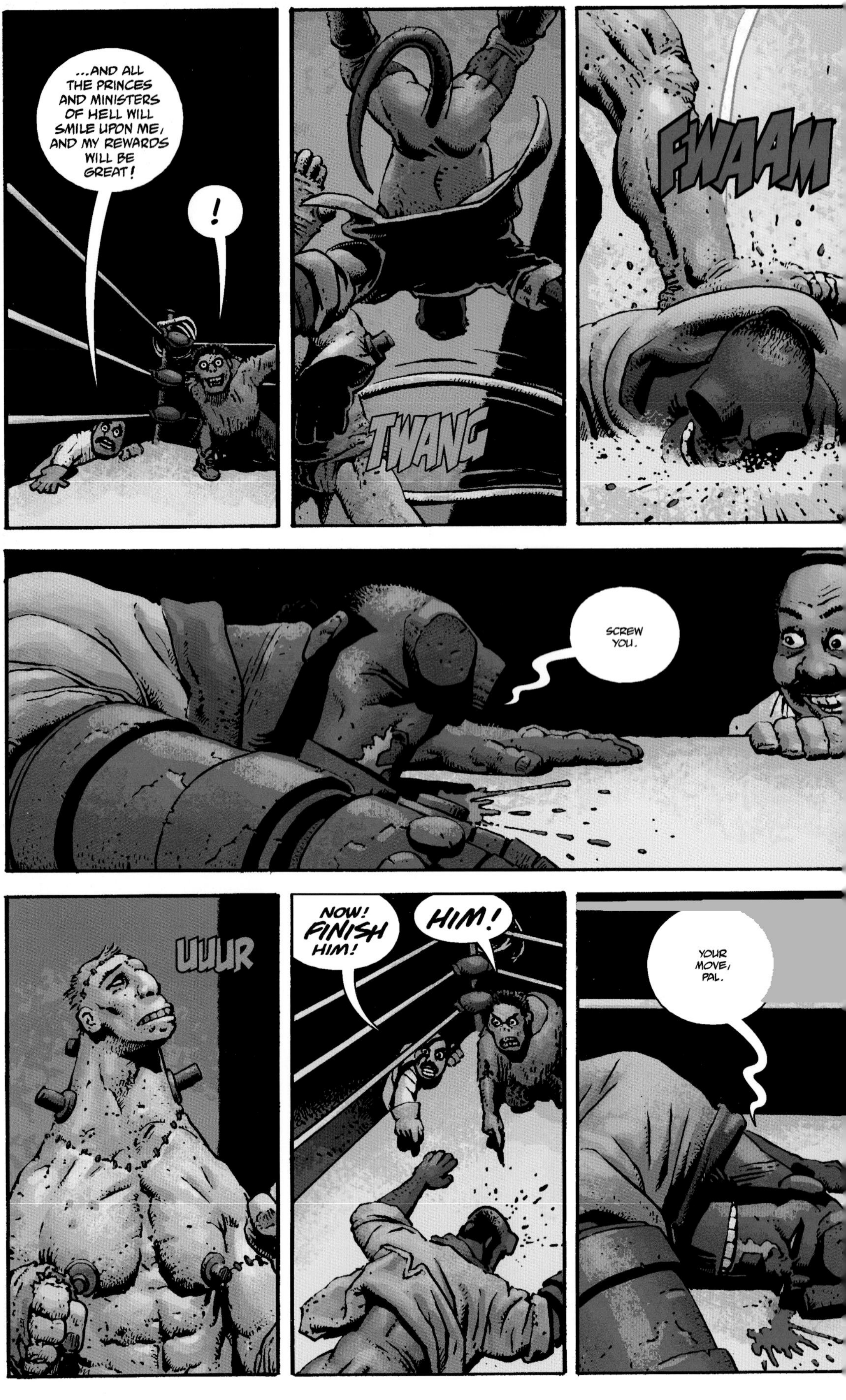
...AND ALL THE PRINCES AND MINISTERS OF HELL WILL SMILE UPON ME, AND MY REWARDS WILL BE GREAT!
!
TWANG
FWAAM
SCREW YOU.
UUUR
NOW! FINISH HIM!
HIM!
YOUR MOVE, PAL.

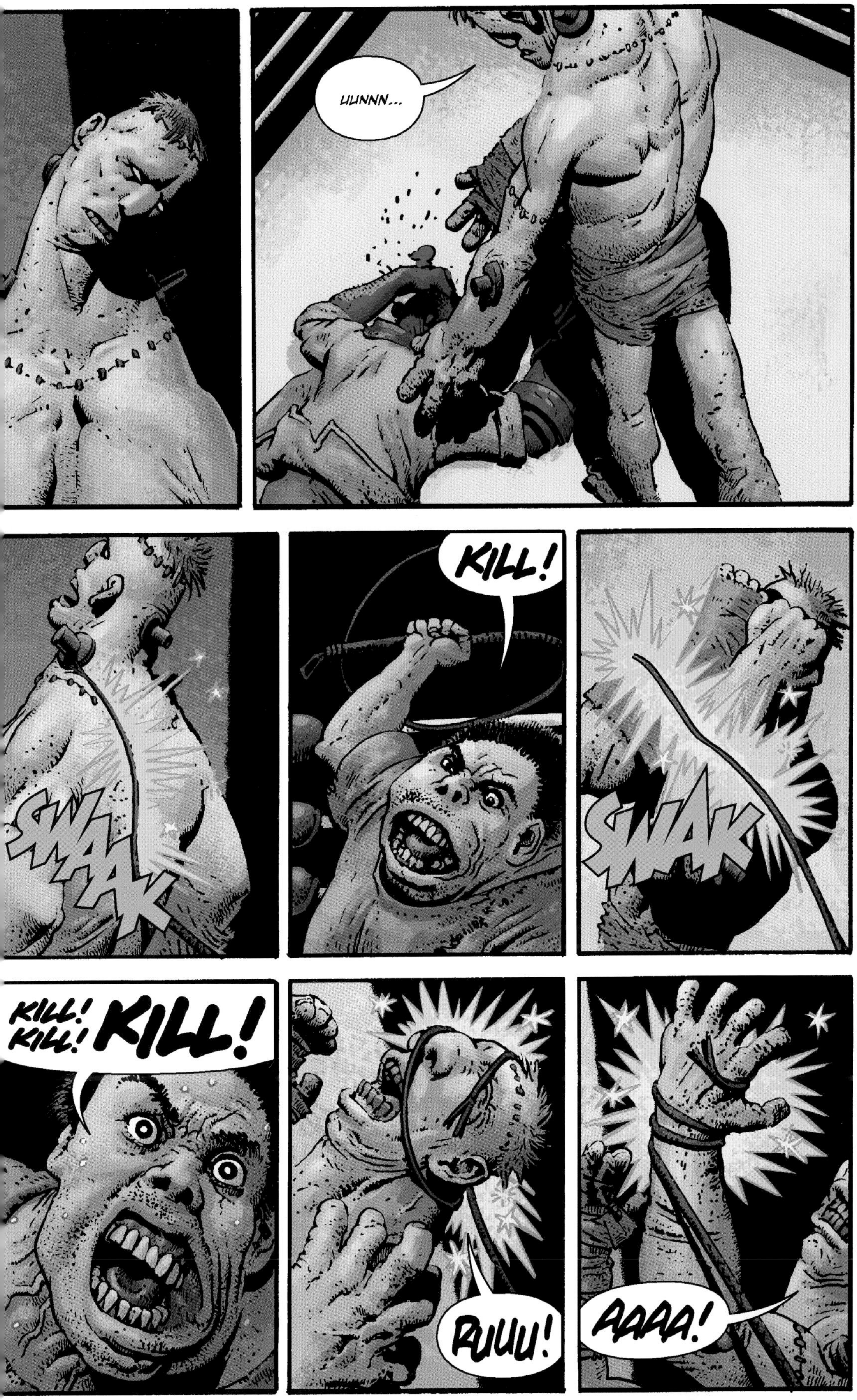
UUNNN...
SWAK
KILL!
SWAK
KILL! KILL! KILL!
RUUU!
AAAA!

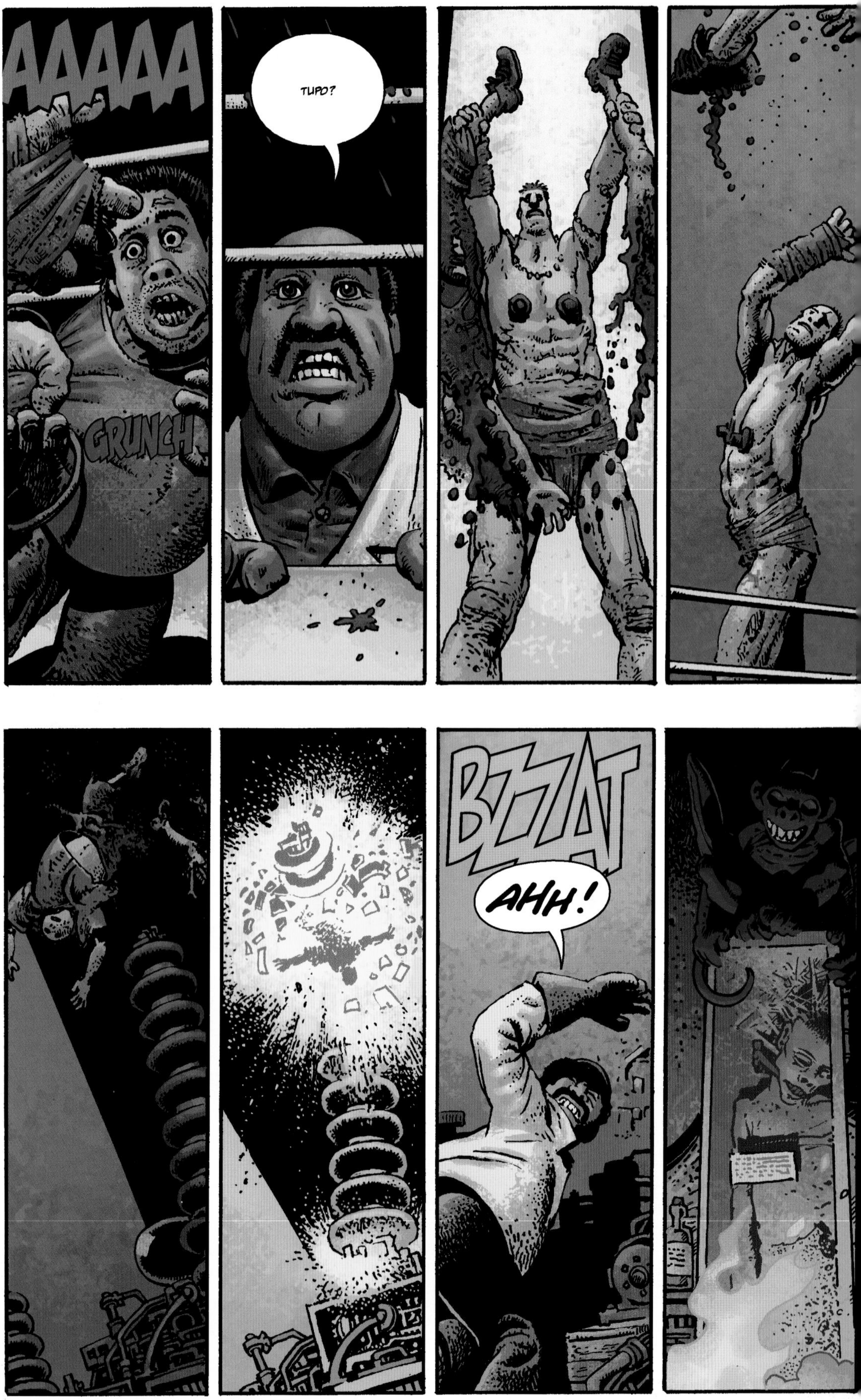
AAAAA
GRUNCH
TUPO?
BZZAT
AHH!

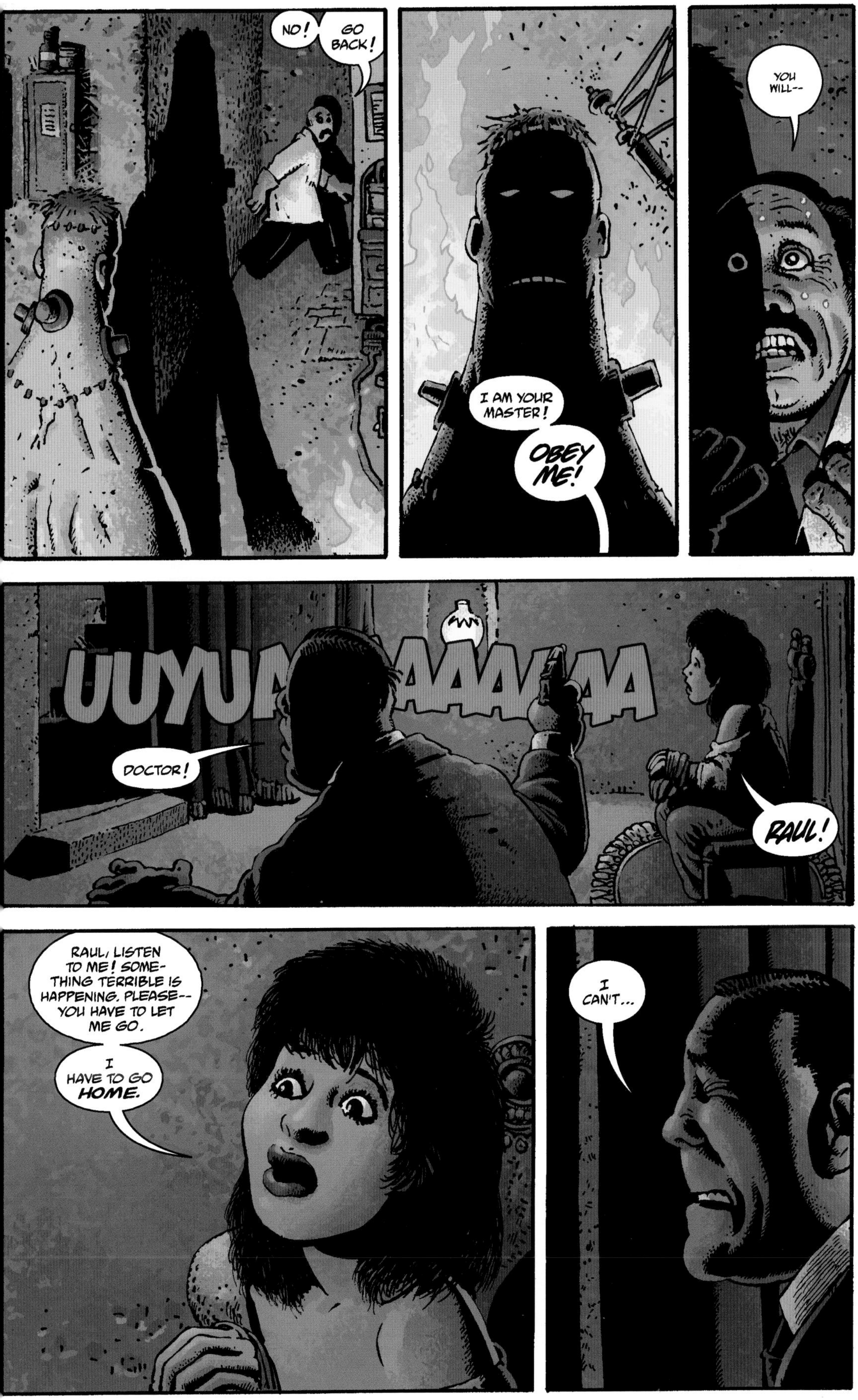
NO!
GO BACK!
I AM YOUR MASTER!
OBEY ME!
YOU WILL--
UUYUAAAAAAA
DOCTOR!
RAUL!
RAUL, LISTEN TO ME! SOME- THING TERRIBLE IS HAPPENING. PLEASE-- YOU HAVE TO LET ME GO.
I HAVE TO GO HOME.
I CAN'T...

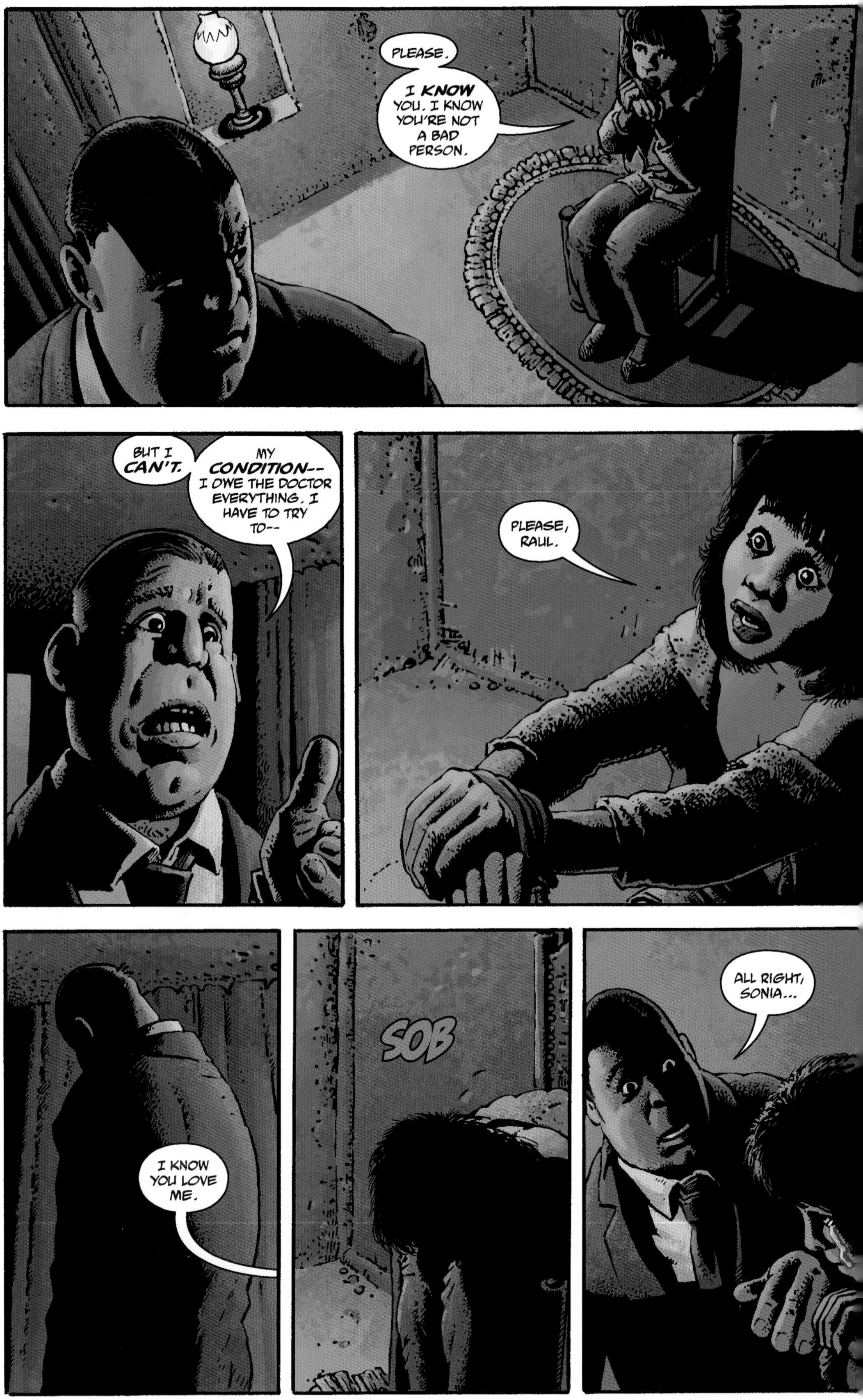
PLEASE.
I KNOW YOU. I KNOW YOU'RE NOT A BAD PERSON.
BUT I CAN'T.
MY CONDITION-- I OWE THE DOCTOR EVERYTHING. I HAVE TO TRY TO--
PLEASE, RAUL.
I KNOW YOU LOVE ME.
SOB
ALL RIGHT, SONIA...

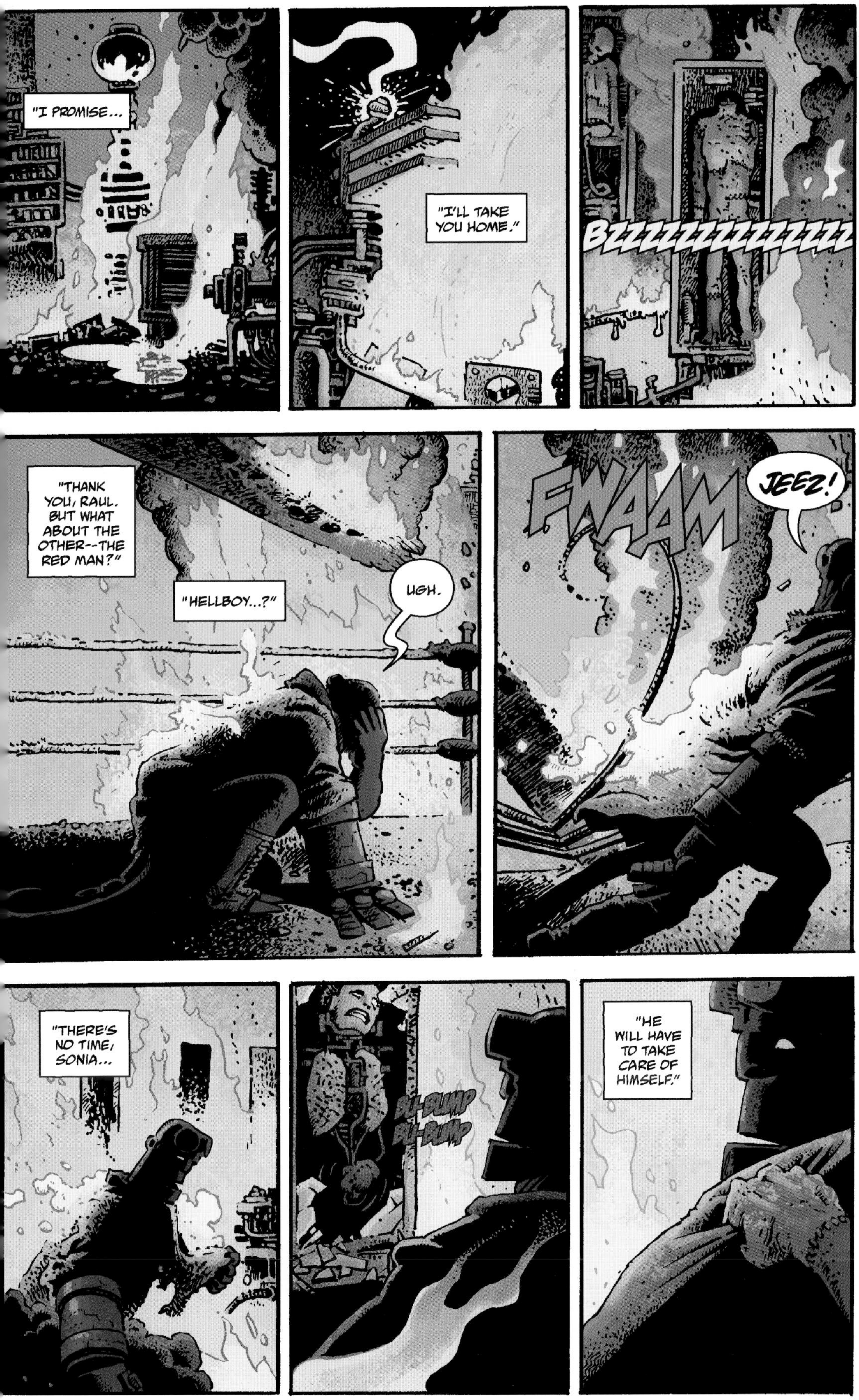

"I PROMISE...
"I'LL TAKE YOU HOME."
BZZZZZZZZZZZZZZ
"THANK YOU, RAUL. BUT WHAT ABOUT THE OTHER--THE RED MAN?"
"HELLBOY...?"
UGH.
FWAAM
JEEZ!
"THERE'S NO TIME, SONIA...
BU-BUMP BU-BUMP
"HE WILL HAVE TO TAKE CARE OF HIMSELF."

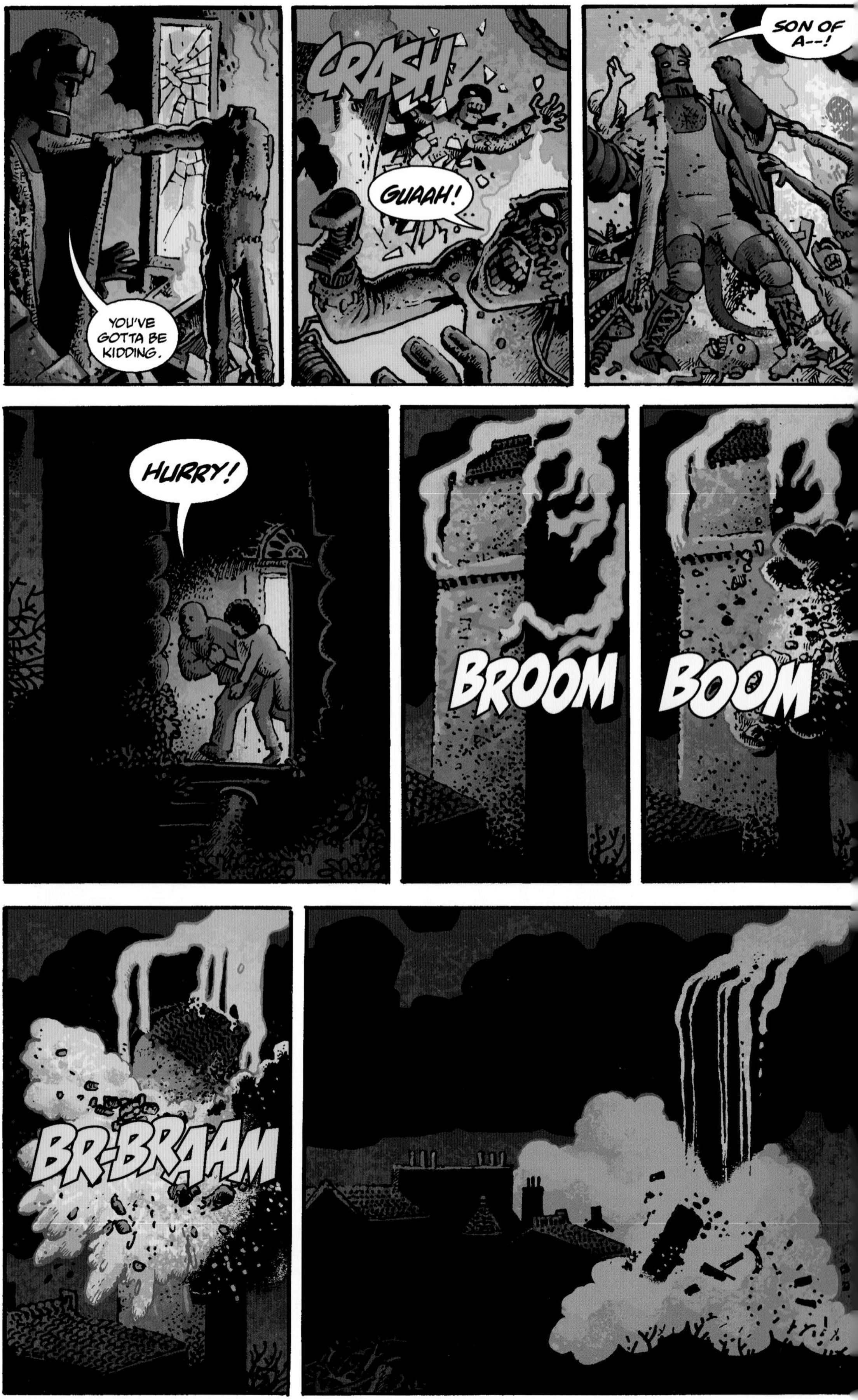
YOU'VE GOTTA BE KIDDING.
CRASH
GUAAH!
SON OF A--!
HURRY!
BROOM
BOOM
BR-BRAAM

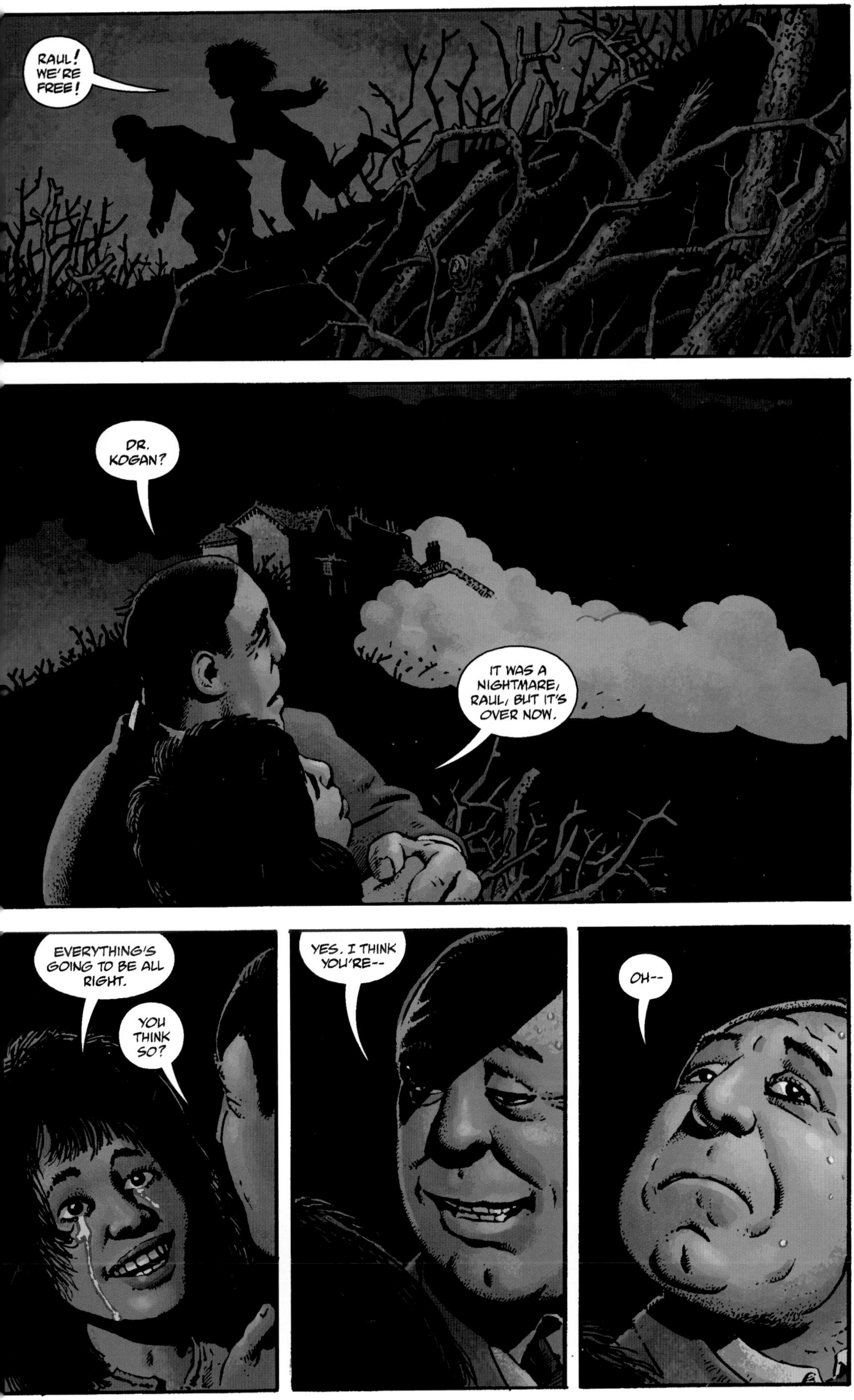
RAUL! WE'RE FREE!
DR. KOGAN?
IT WAS A NIGHTMARE, RAUL, BUT IT'S OVER NOW.
EVERYTHING'S GOING TO BE ALL RIGHT.
YOU THINK SO?
YES. I THINK YOU'RE--
OH--

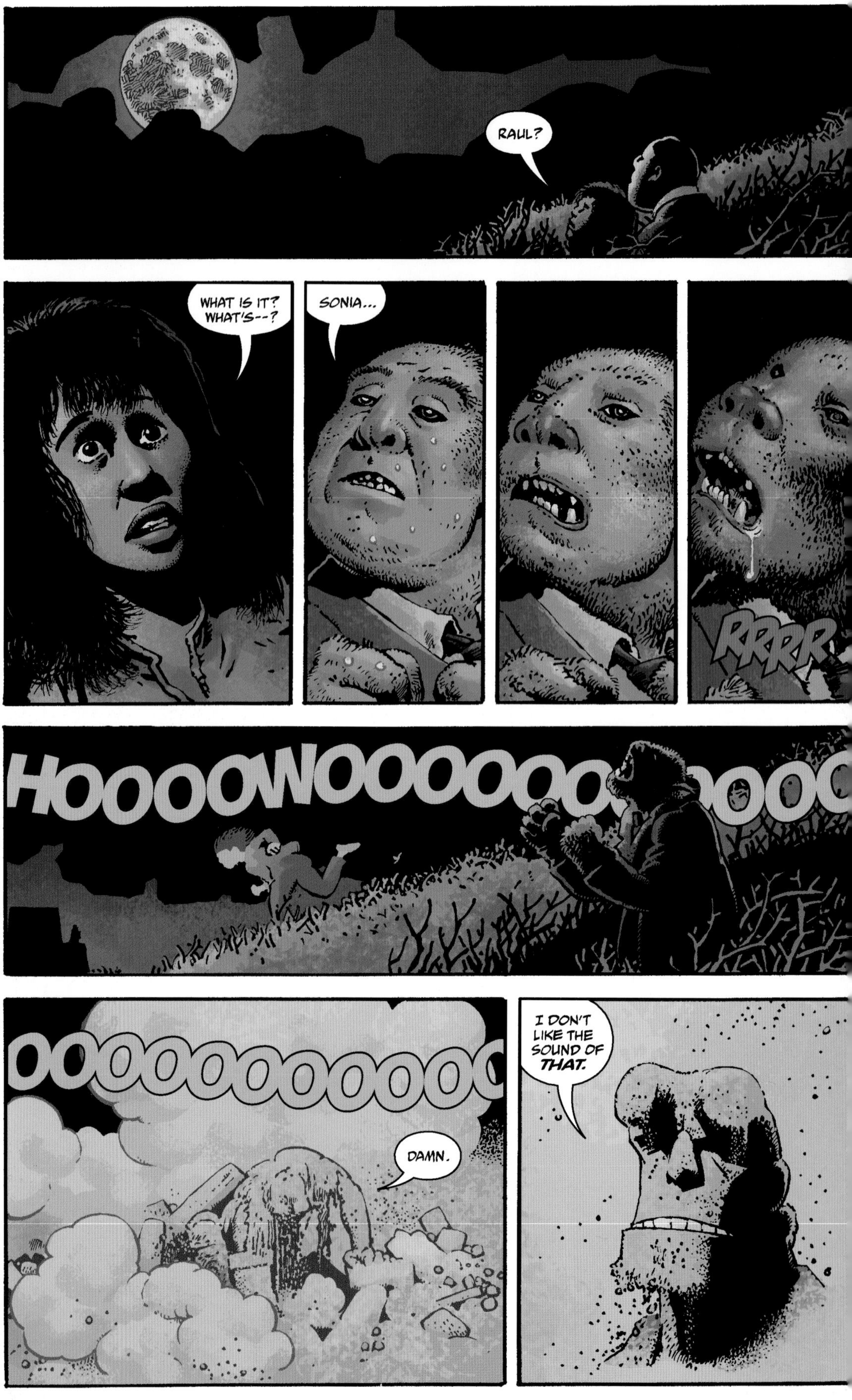
RAUL?
WHAT IS IT? WHAT'S--?
SONIA...
RRRR
HOOOOWOOOOOOOOOOOO
OOOOOOOOOOOO
DAMN.
I DON'T LIKE THE SOUND OF *THAT.*

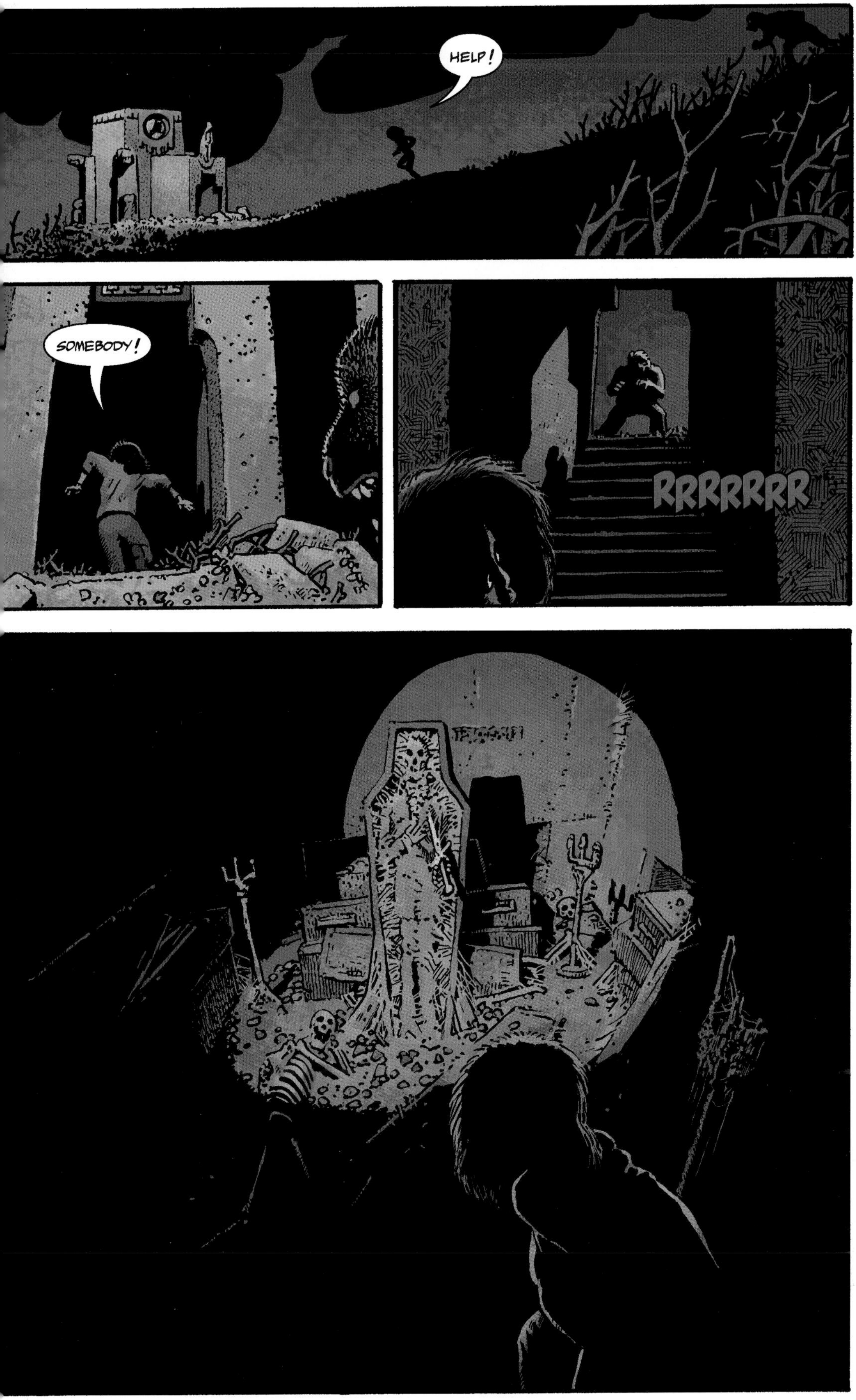
HELP!
SOMEBODY!
RRRRRRR

HELLBOY

by MIKE MIGNOLA

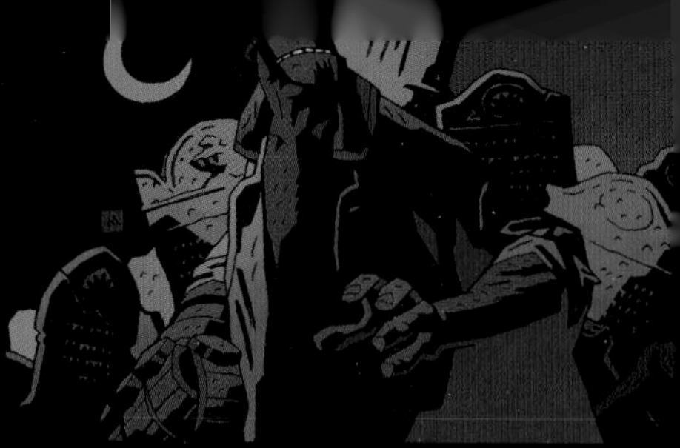

HELLBOY LIBRARY EDITION VOLUME 1:
SEED OF DESTRUCTION AND WAKE THE DEVIL
ISBN 978-1-59307-910-9 | $49.99

HELLBOY LIBRARY EDITION VOLUME 2:
THE CHAINED COFFIN AND THE RIGHT HAND OF DOOM
ISBN 978-1-59307-989-5 | $49.99

HELLBOY LIBRARY EDITION VOLUME 3:
CONQUEROR WORM AND STRANGE PLACES
ISBN 978-1-59582-352-6 | $49.99

HELLBOY LIBRARY EDITION VOLUME 4:
THE CROOKED MAN AND THE TROLL WITCH
WITH RICHARD CORBEN AND OTHERS
ISBN 978-1-59582-658-9 | $49.99

SEED OF DESTRUCTION
WITH JOHN BYRNE
ISBN 978-1-59307-094-6 | $17.99

WAKE THE DEVIL
ISBN 978-1-59307-095-3 | $17.99

THE CHAINED COFFIN AND OTHERS
ISBN 978-1-59307-091-5 | $17.99

THE RIGHT HAND OF DOOM
ISBN 978-1-59307-093-9 | $17.99

CONQUEROR WORM
ISBN 978-1-59307-092-2 | $17.99

STRANGE PLACES
ISBN 978-1-59307-475-3 | $17.99

THE TROLL WITCH AND OTHERS
ISBN 978-1-59307-860-7 | $17.99

DARKNESS CALLS
WITH DUNCAN FEGREDO
ISBN 978-1-59307-896-6 | $19.99

THE WILD HUNT
WITH DUNCAN FEGREDO
ISBN 978-1-59582-352-6 | $19.99

THE CROOKED MAN AND OTHERS
WITH RICHARD CORBEN
ISBN 978-1-59582-477-6 | $17.99

THE BRIDE OF HELL AND OTHERS
WITH RICHARD CORBEN, KEVIN NOWLAN, AND SCOTT HAMPTON
ISBN 978-1-59582-740-1 | $19.99

THE ART OF HELLBOY
ISBN 978-1-59307-089-2 | $29.99

HELLBOY II: THE ART OF THE MOVIE
ISBN 978-1-59307-964-2 | $24.99

HELLBOY: THE COMPANION
ISBN 978-1-59307-655-9 | $14.99

HELLBOY: WEIRD TALES
VOLUME 1
ISBN 978-1-56971-622-9 | $17.99
VOLUME 2
ISBN 978-1-56971-953-4 | $17.99

HELLBOY: MASKS AND MONSTERS
WITH JAMES ROBINSON AND SCOTT BENEFIEL
ISBN 978-1-59582-567-4 | $17.99

B.P.R.D.

WITH JOHN ARCUDI AND GUY DAVIS

PLAGUE OF FROGS HARDCOVER COLLECTION VOLUME 1
ISBN 978-59582-609-1 | $34.99

THE DEAD
ISBN 978-1-59307-380-0 | $17.99

THE BLACK FLAME
ISBN 978-1-59307-550-7 | $17.99

WAR ON FROGS
ISBN 978-1-59582-480-6 | $17.99

THE UNIVERSAL MACHINE
ISBN 978-1-59307-710-5 | $17.99

THE GARDEN OF SOULS
ISBN 978-1-59307-882-9 | $17.99

KILLING GROUND
ISBN 978-1-59307-956-7 | $17.99

THE WARNING
ISBN 978-1-59582-304-5 | $17.99

THE BLACK GODDESS
ISBN 978-1-59582-411-0 | $17.99

KING OF FEAR
ISBN 978-1-59582-564-3 | $17.99

1946
WITH JOSHUA DYSART AND PAUL AZACETA
ISBN 978-1-59582-191-1 | $17.99

1947
WITH JOSHUA DYSART, FÁBIO MOON, AND GABRIEL BÁ
ISBN 978-1-59582-478-3 | $17.99

B.P.R.D. HELL ON EARTH VOLUME 1: NEW WORLD
ISBN 978-1-59582-707-4 | $19.99

ABE SAPIEN: THE DROWNING
WITH JASON SHAWN ALEXANDER
ISBN 978-1-59582-185-0 | $17.99

LOBSTER JOHNSON: THE IRON PROMETHEUS
WITH JASON ARMSTRONG
ISBN 978-1-59307-975-8 | $17.99

WITCHFINDER: IN THE SERVICE OF ANGELS
WITH BEN STENBECK
ISBN 978-1-59582-483-7 | $17.99

NOVELS

HELLBOY: EMERALD HELL
BY TOM PICCIRILLI
ISBN 978-1-59582-141-6 | $12.99

HELLBOY: THE ALL-SEEING EYE
BY MARK MORRIS
ISBN 978-1-59582-141-6 | $12.99

HELLBOY: THE FIRE WOLVES
BY TIM LEBBON
ISBN 978-1-59582-204-8 | $12.99

HELLBOY: THE ICE WOLVES
BY MARK CHADBOURN
ISBN 978-1-59582-205-5 | $12.99

LOBSTER JOHNSON: THE SATAN FACTORY
BY THOMAS E. SNIEGOSKI
ISBN 978-1-59582-203-1 | $12.99

SHORT STORIES

ILLUSTRATED BY MIKE MIGNOLA

HELLBOY: ODD JOBS
BY POPPY Z. BRITE, GREG RUCKA, AND OTHERS
ISBN 978-1-56971-440-9 | $14.99

HELLBOY: ODDER JOBS
BY FRANK DARABONT, GUILLERMO DEL TORO, AND OTHERS
ISBN 978-1-59307-226-1 | $14.99

HELLBOY: ODDEST JOBS
BY JOE R. LANSDALE, CHINA MIÉVILLE, AND OTHERS
ISBN 978-1-59307-944-4 | $14.99

ALSO

THE AMAZING SCREW-ON HEAD AND OTHER CURIOUS OBJECTS HARDCOVER COLLECTION
BY MIKE MIGNOLA
ISBN 978-1-59582-501-8 | $17.99

BALTIMORE: THE PLAGUE SHIPS
WITH CHRISTOPHER GOLDEN AND BEN STENBECK
ISBN 978-1-59582-673-2 | $24.99

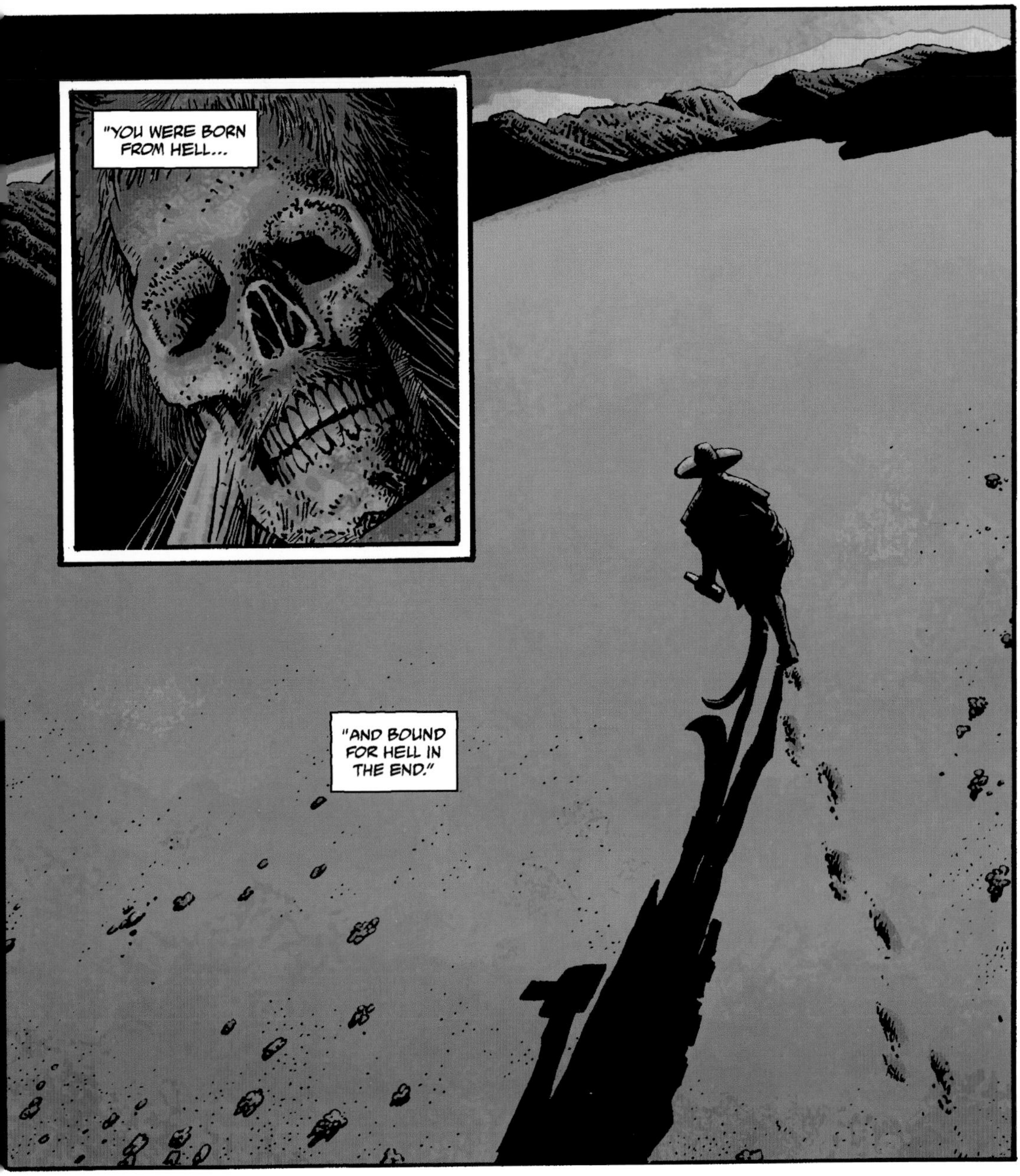
"YOU WERE BORN FROM HELL...
"AND BOUND FOR HELL IN THE END."

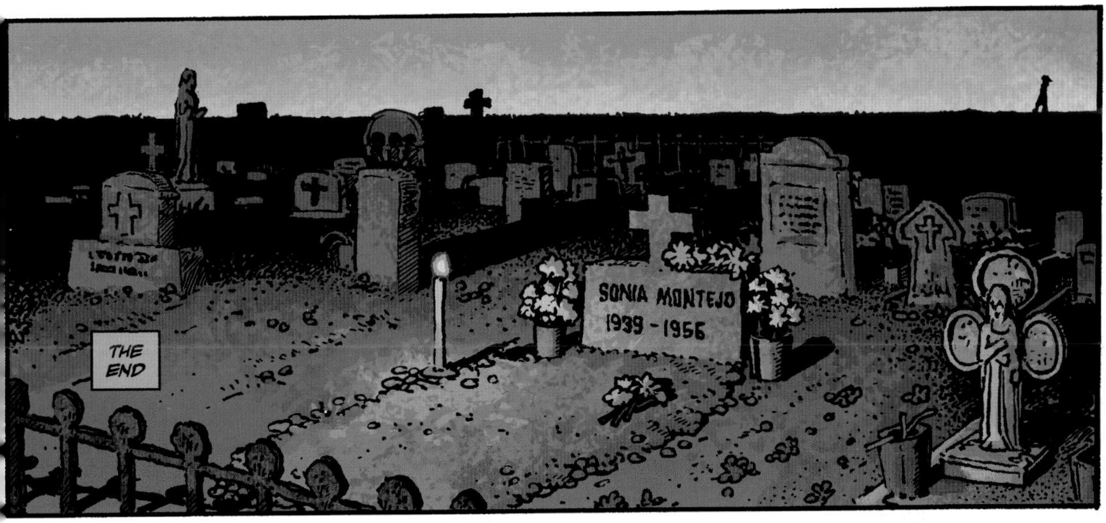
SONIA MONTEJO
1939 - 1956
THE END

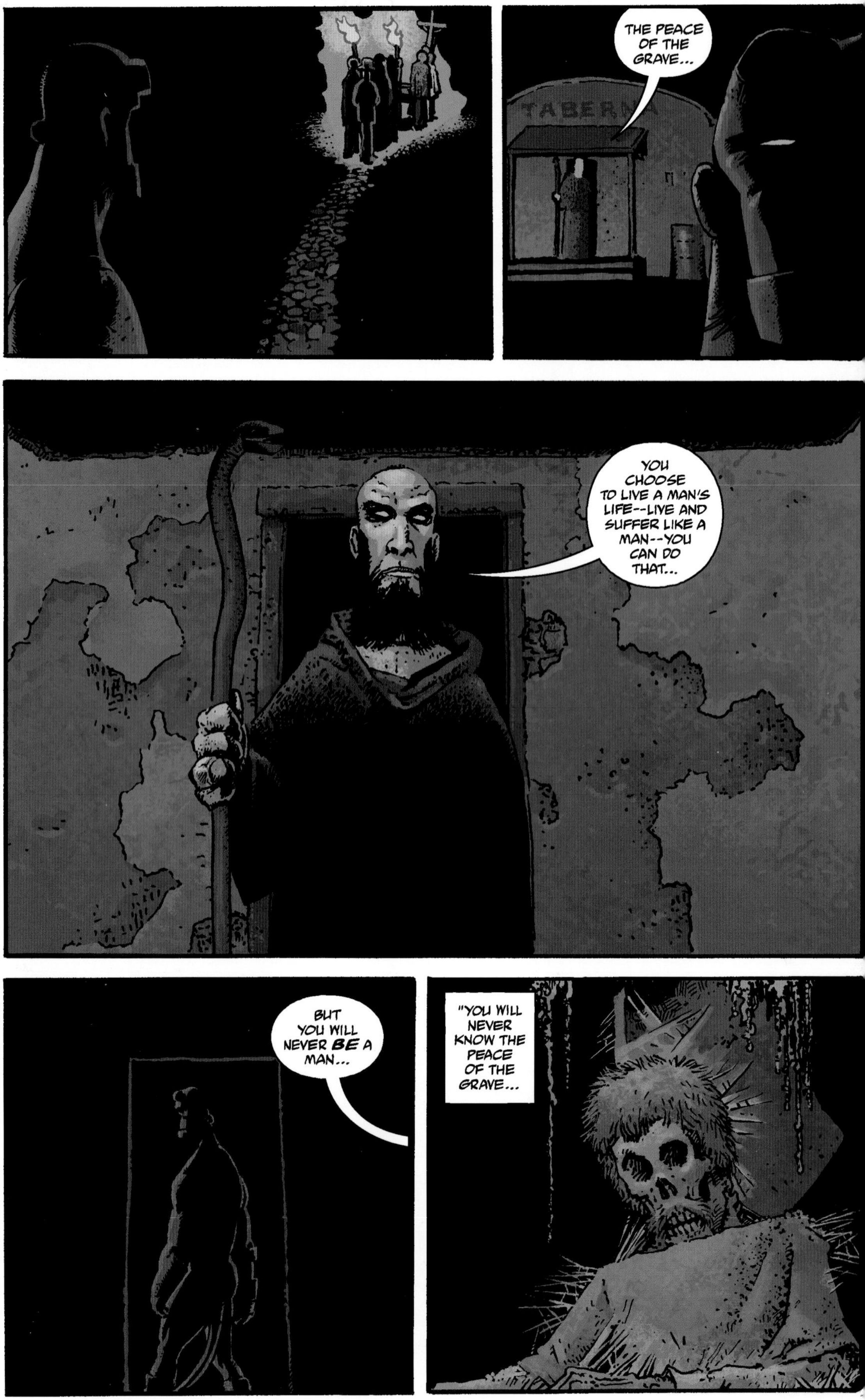
THE PEACE OF THE GRAVE...
YOU CHOOSE TO LIVE A MAN'S LIFE--LIVE AND SUFFER LIKE A MAN--YOU CAN DO THAT...
BUT YOU WILL NEVER BE A MAN...
"YOU WILL NEVER KNOW THE PEACE OF THE GRAVE...

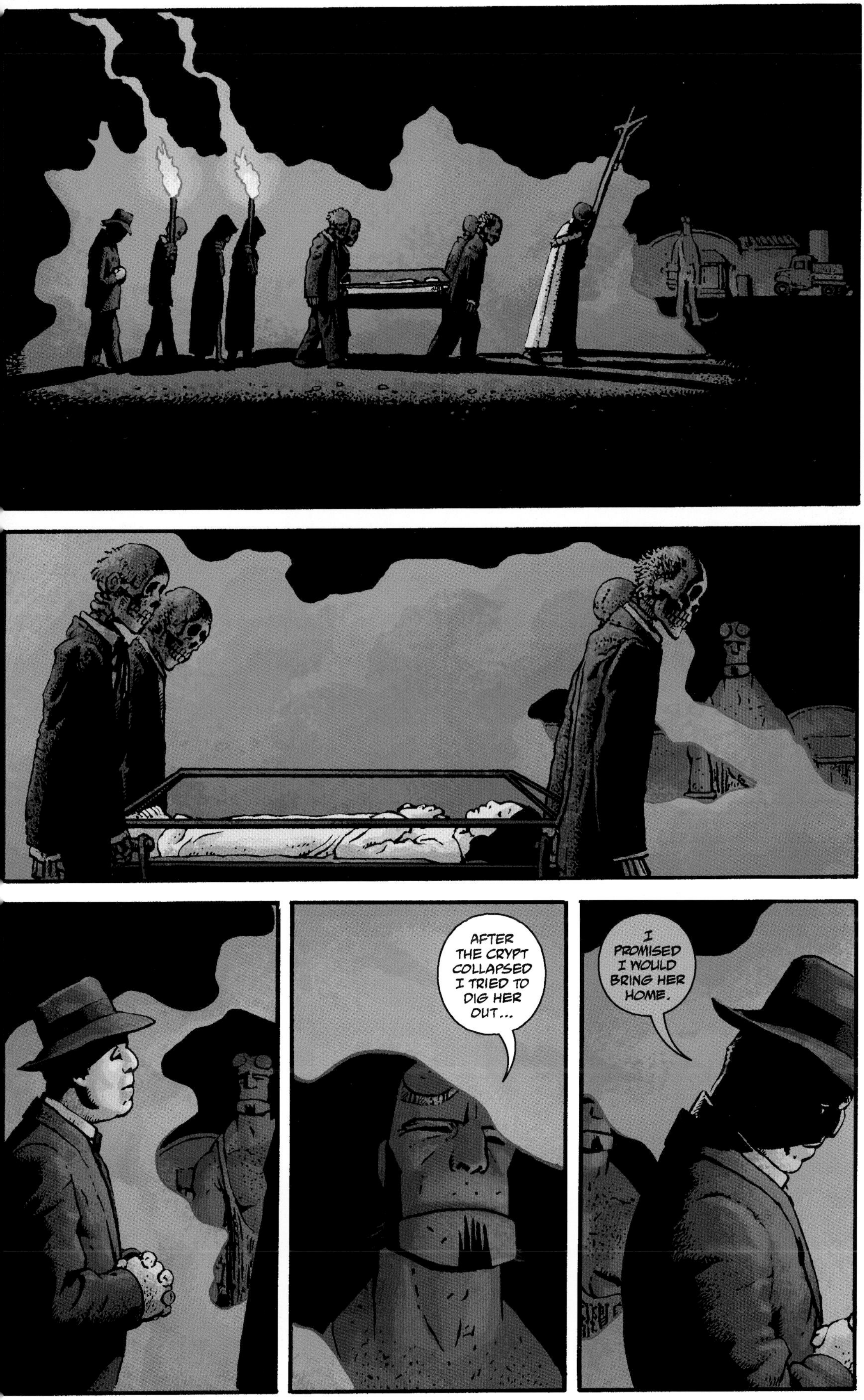
AFTER THE CRYPT COLLAPSED I TRIED TO DIG HER OUT...
I PROMISED I WOULD BRING HER HOME.

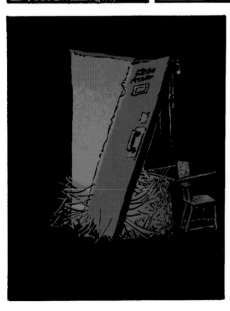
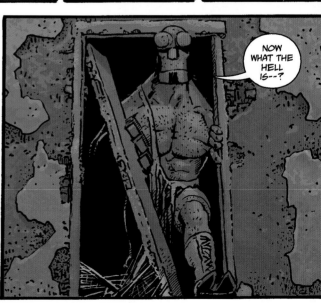

NOW WHAT THE HELL IS--?

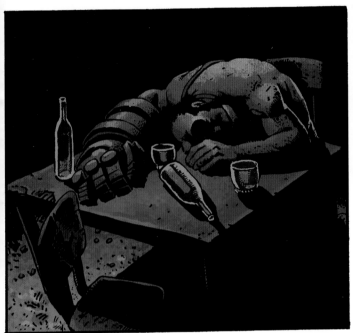

UHH...

CRAP.

"HE SAID HE MADE ME, BUT IT'S NOT TRUE..."

HE BOUGHT ME FROM A CARNIVAL.

I DON'T KNOW WHERE I COME FROM OR WHERE I'M GOING.

AMEN, BROTHER.

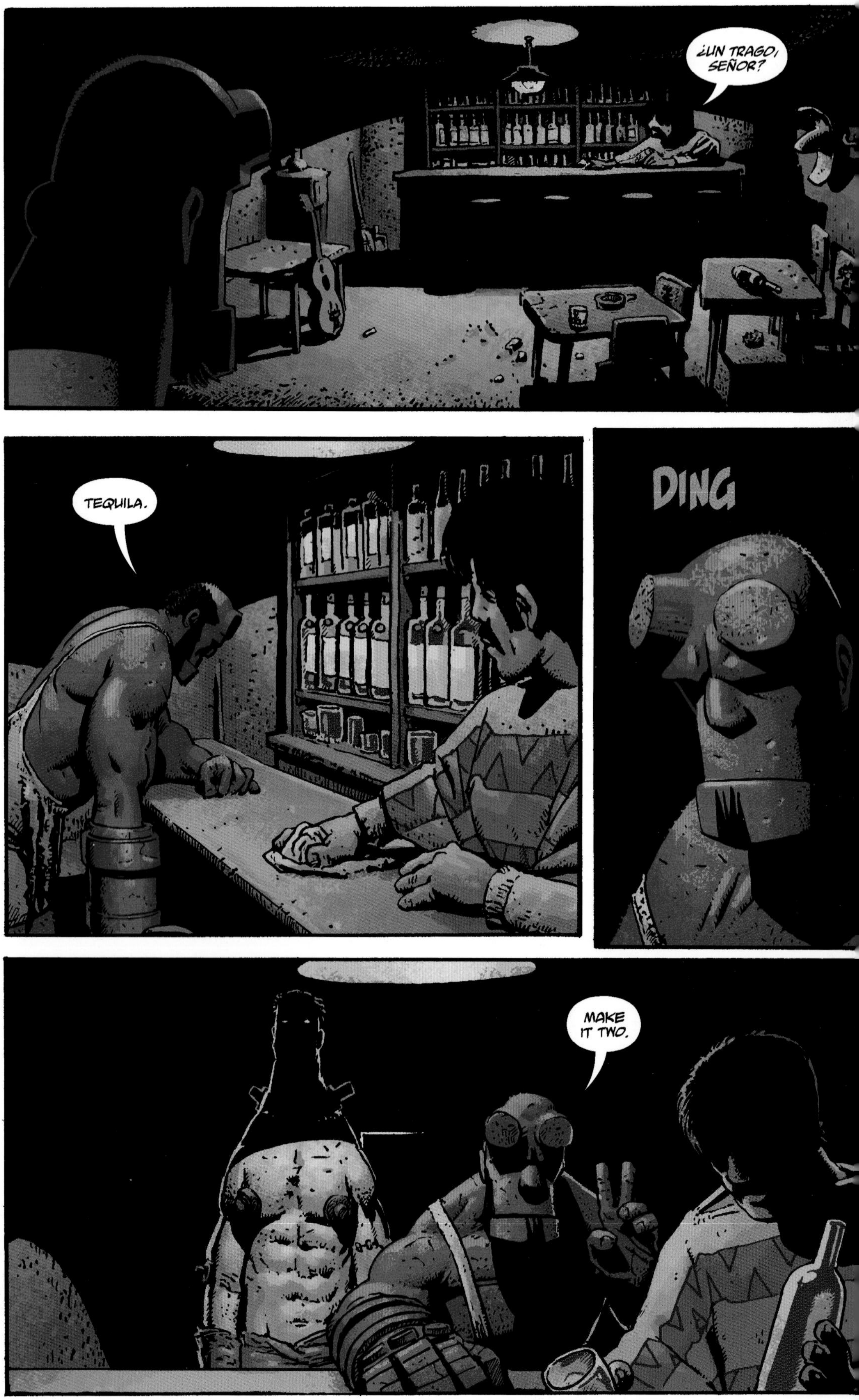
¿UN TRAGO, SEÑOR?
TEQUILA.
DING
MAKE IT TWO.

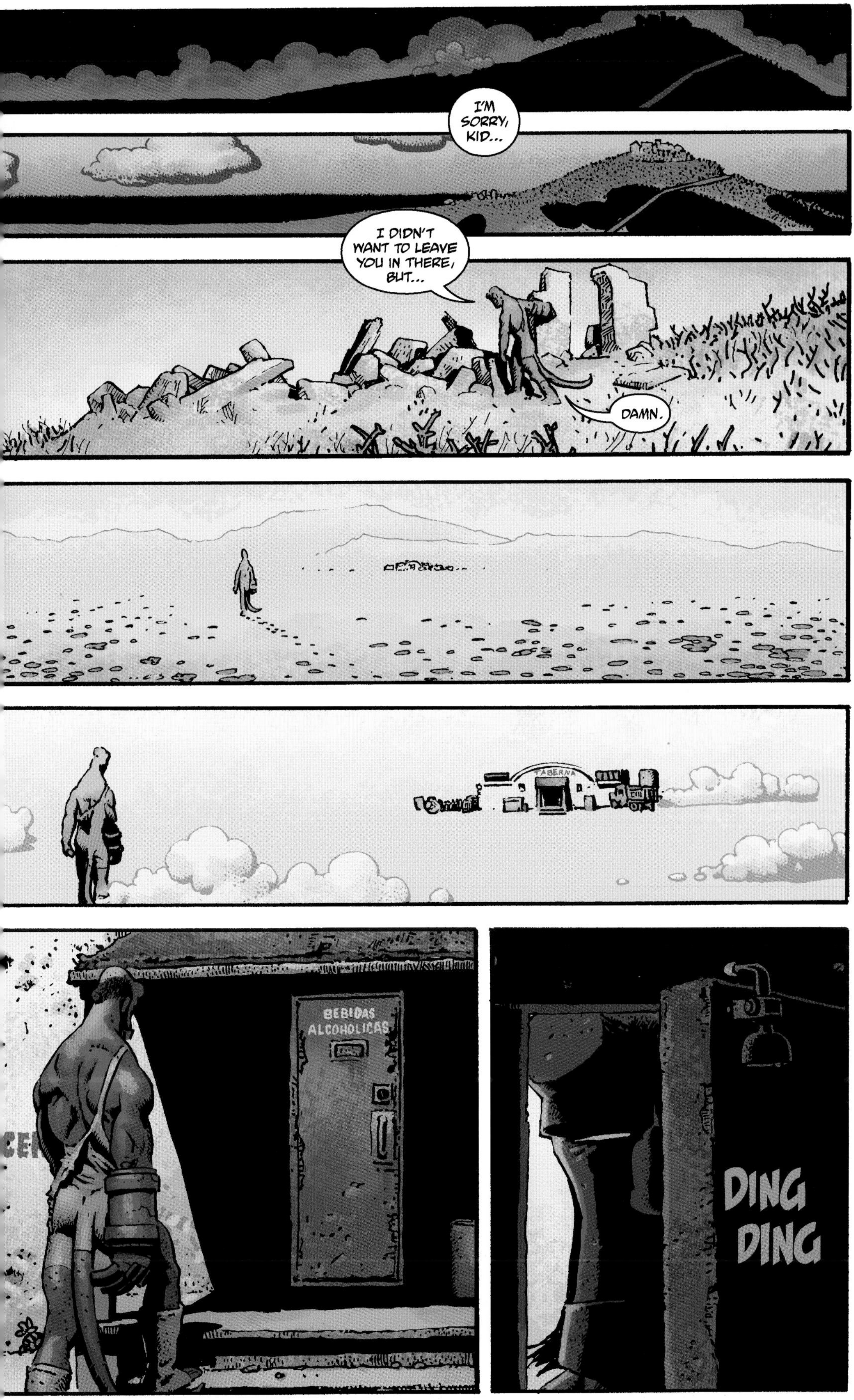
I'M SORRY, KID...
I DIDN'T WANT TO LEAVE YOU IN THERE, BUT...
DAMN.
TABERNA
BEBIDAS ALCOHOLICAS
DING DING

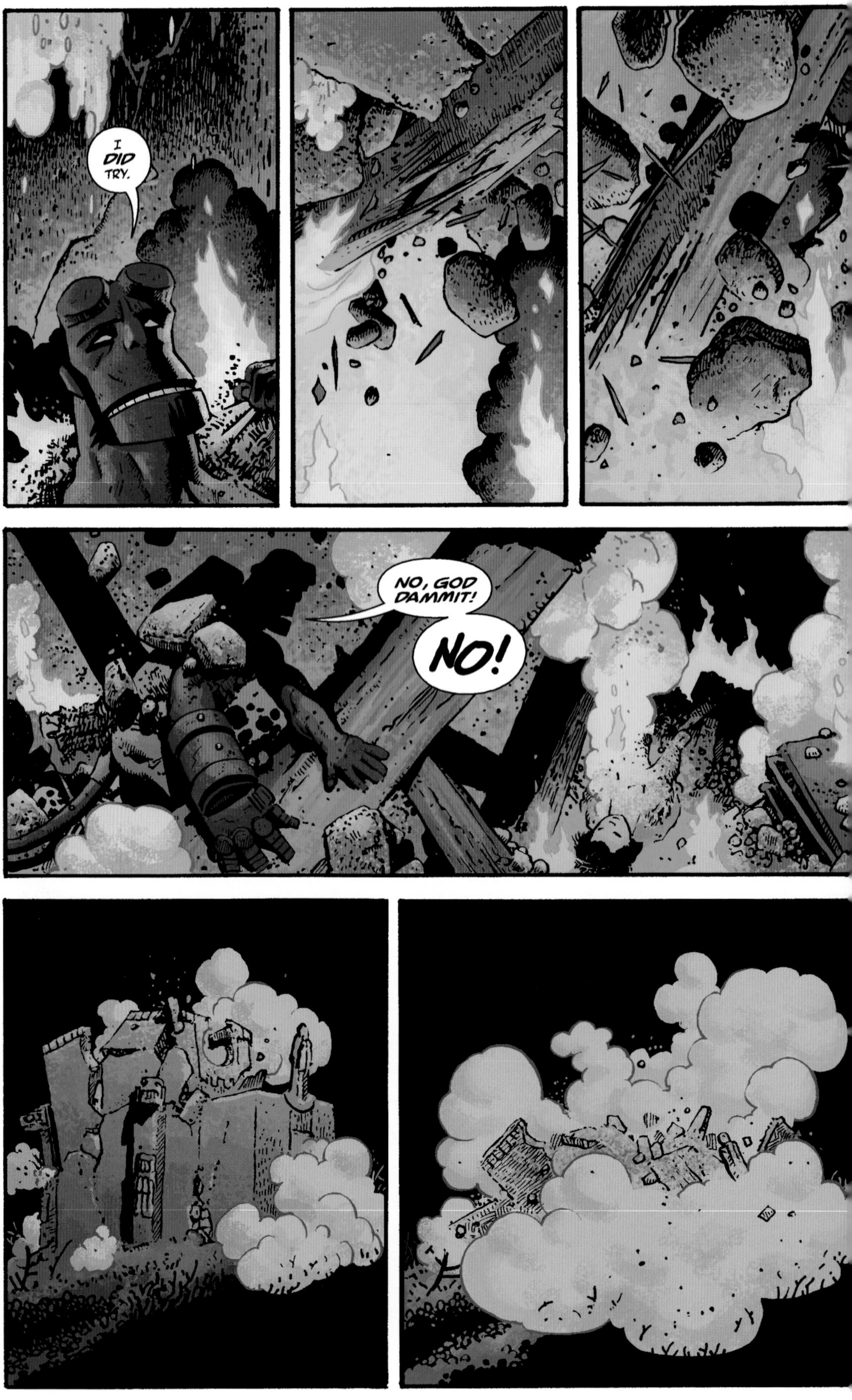
I DID TRY.
NO, GOD DAMMIT!
NO!

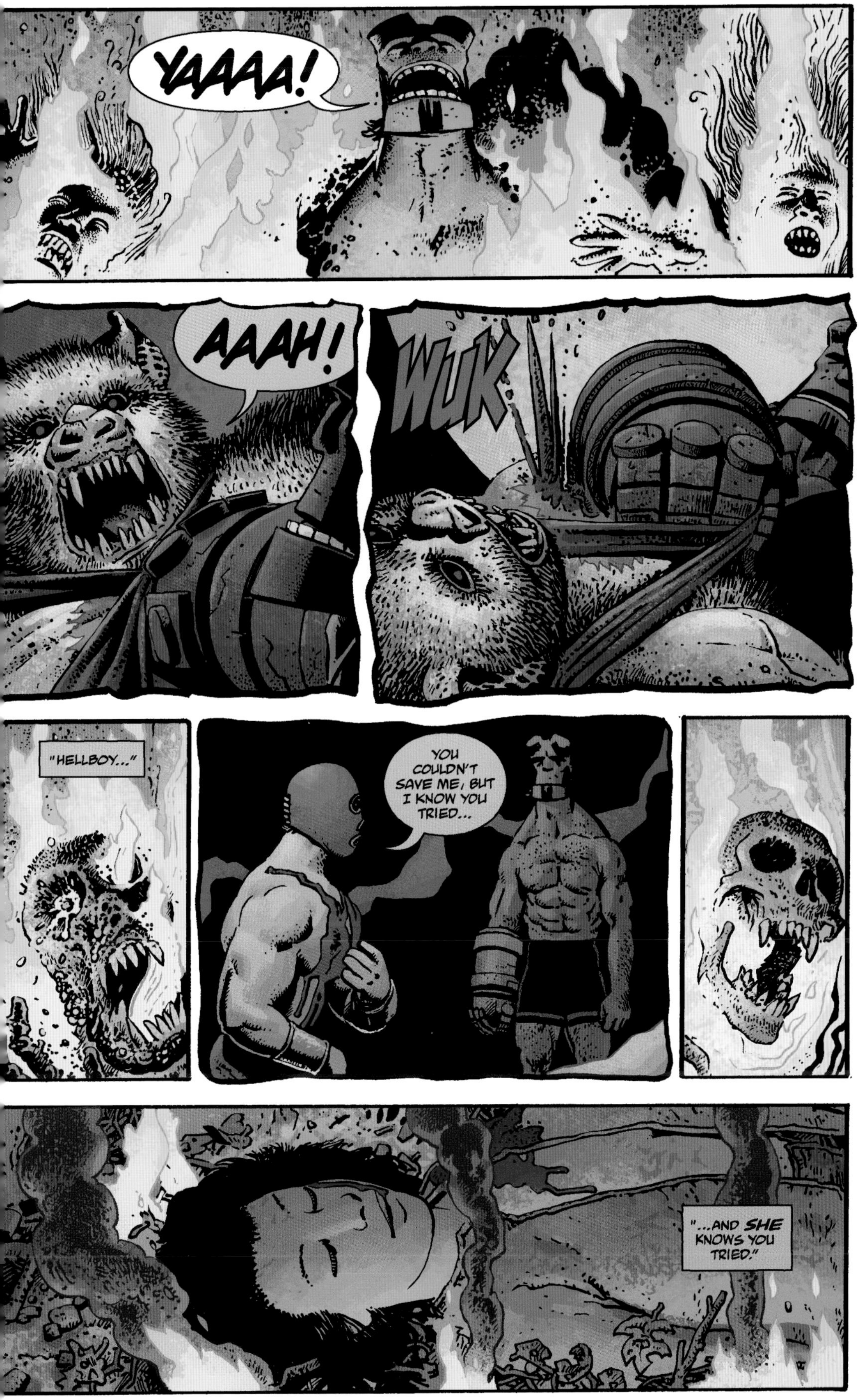
YAAAA!
AAAH!
WUK
"HELLBOY..."
YOU COULDN'T SAVE ME, BUT I KNOW YOU TRIED...
"...AND SHE KNOWS YOU TRIED."

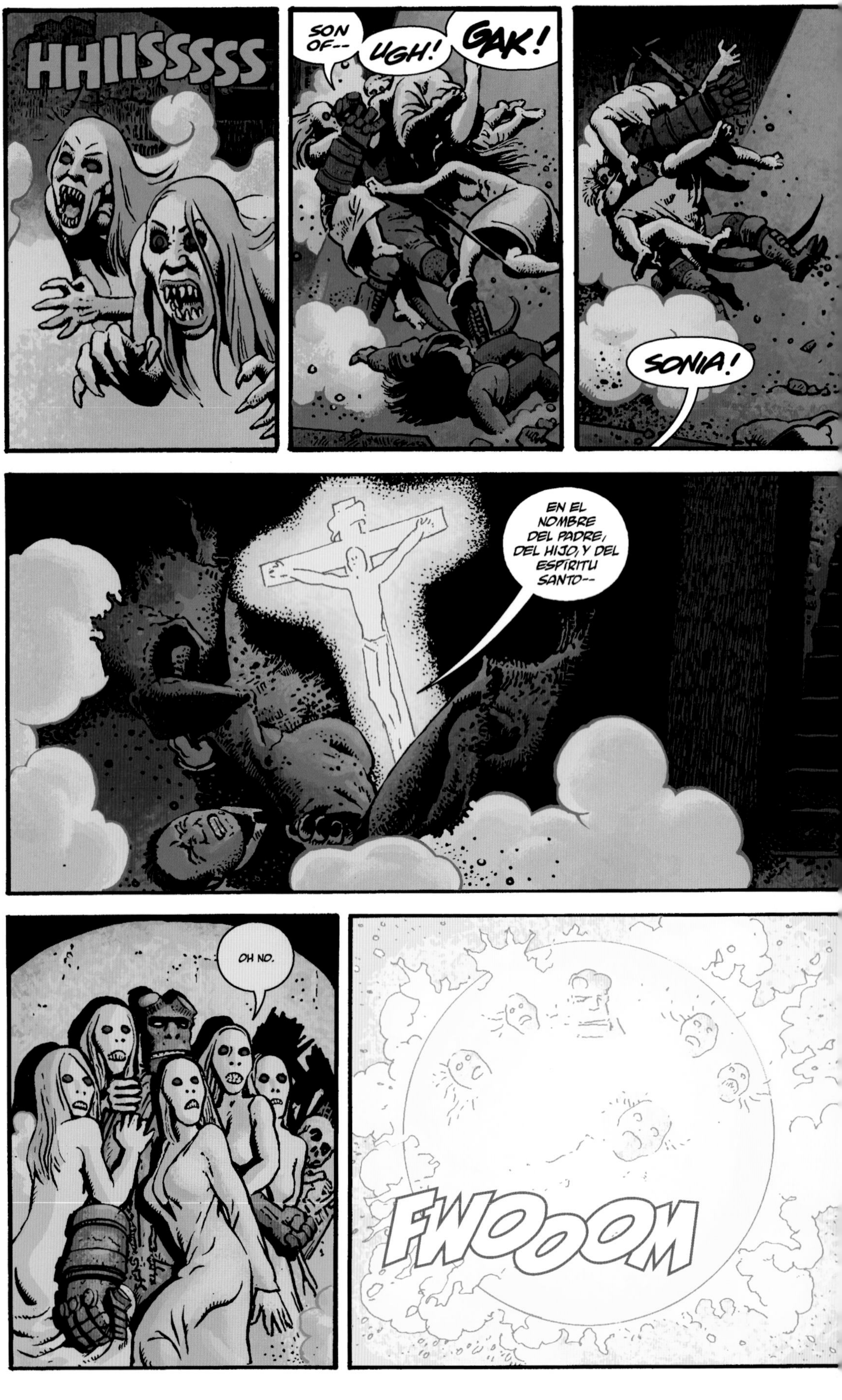
HHIISSSSS
SON OF--
UGH!
GAK!
SONIA!
EN EL NOMBRE DEL PADRE, DEL HIJO, Y DEL ESPIRITU SANTO--
OH NO.
FWOOOOM

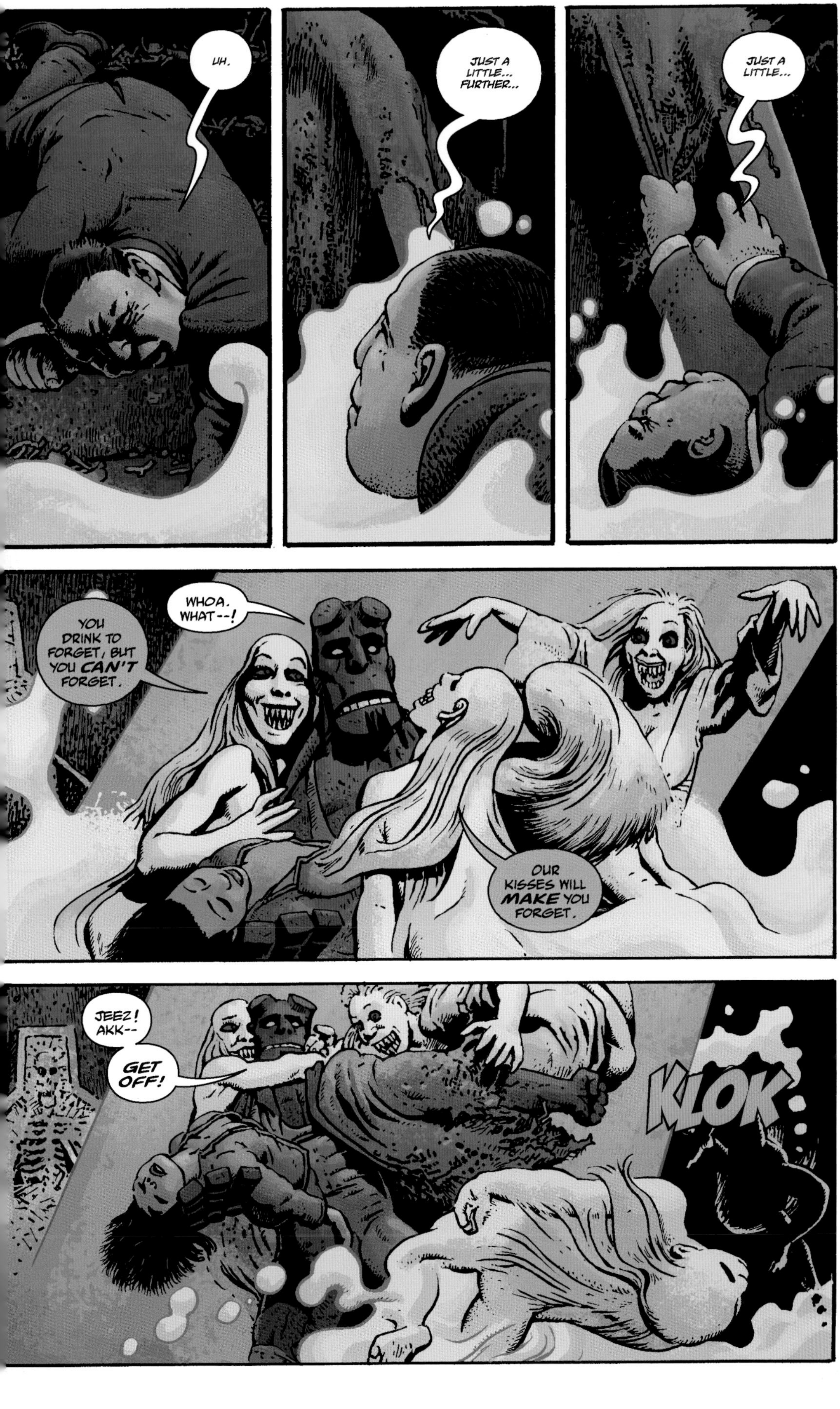
UH.
JUST A LITTLE... FURTHER...
JUST A LITTLE...
YOU DRINK TO FORGET, BUT YOU CAN'T FORGET.
WHOA. WHAT--!
OUR KISSES WILL MAKE YOU FORGET.
JEEZ! AKK--
GET OFF!
KLOK

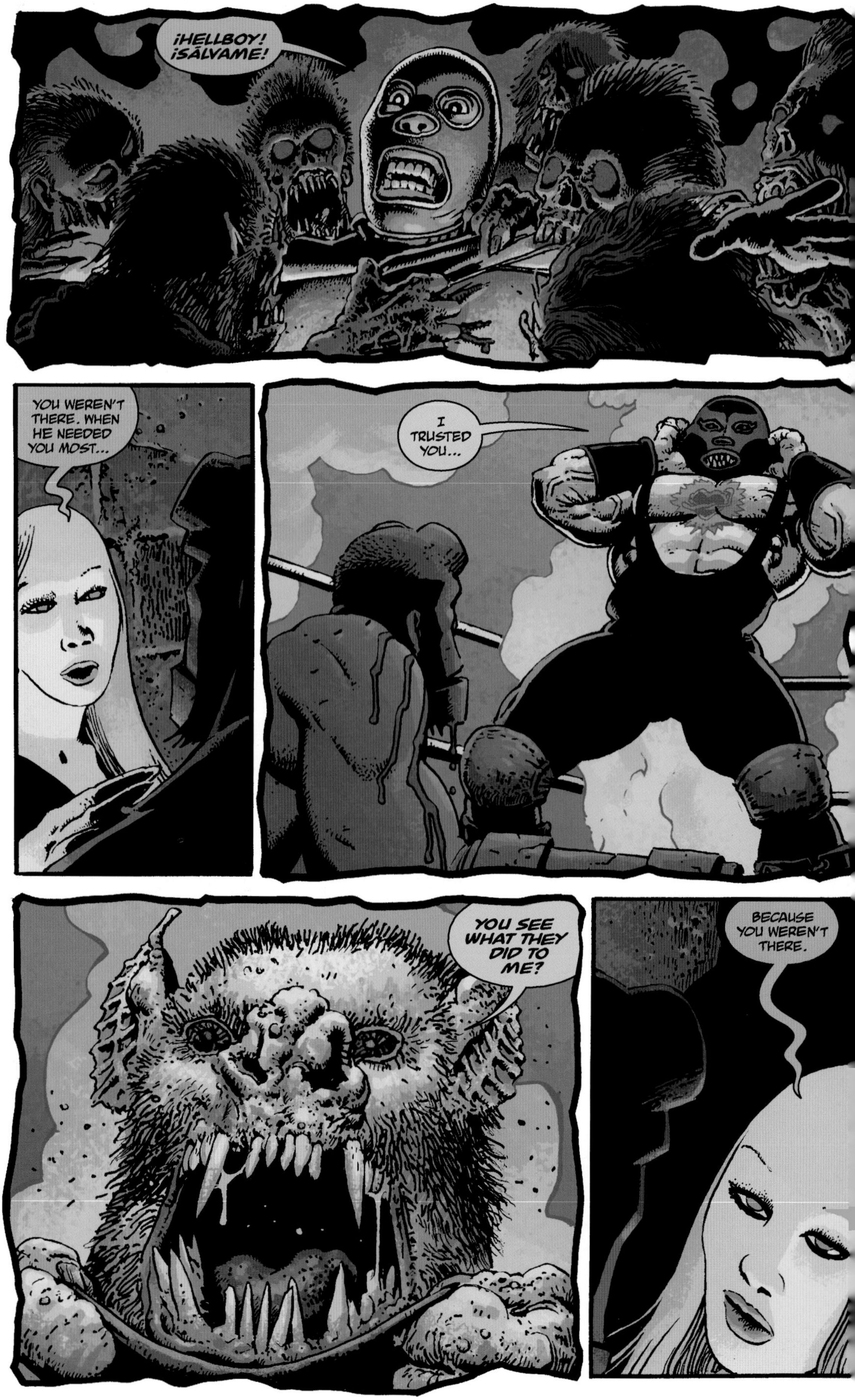
¡HELLBOY! ¡SÁLVAME!
YOU WEREN'T THERE. WHEN HE NEEDED YOU MOST...
I TRUSTED YOU...
YOU SEE WHAT THEY DID TO ME?
BECAUSE YOU WEREN'T THERE.

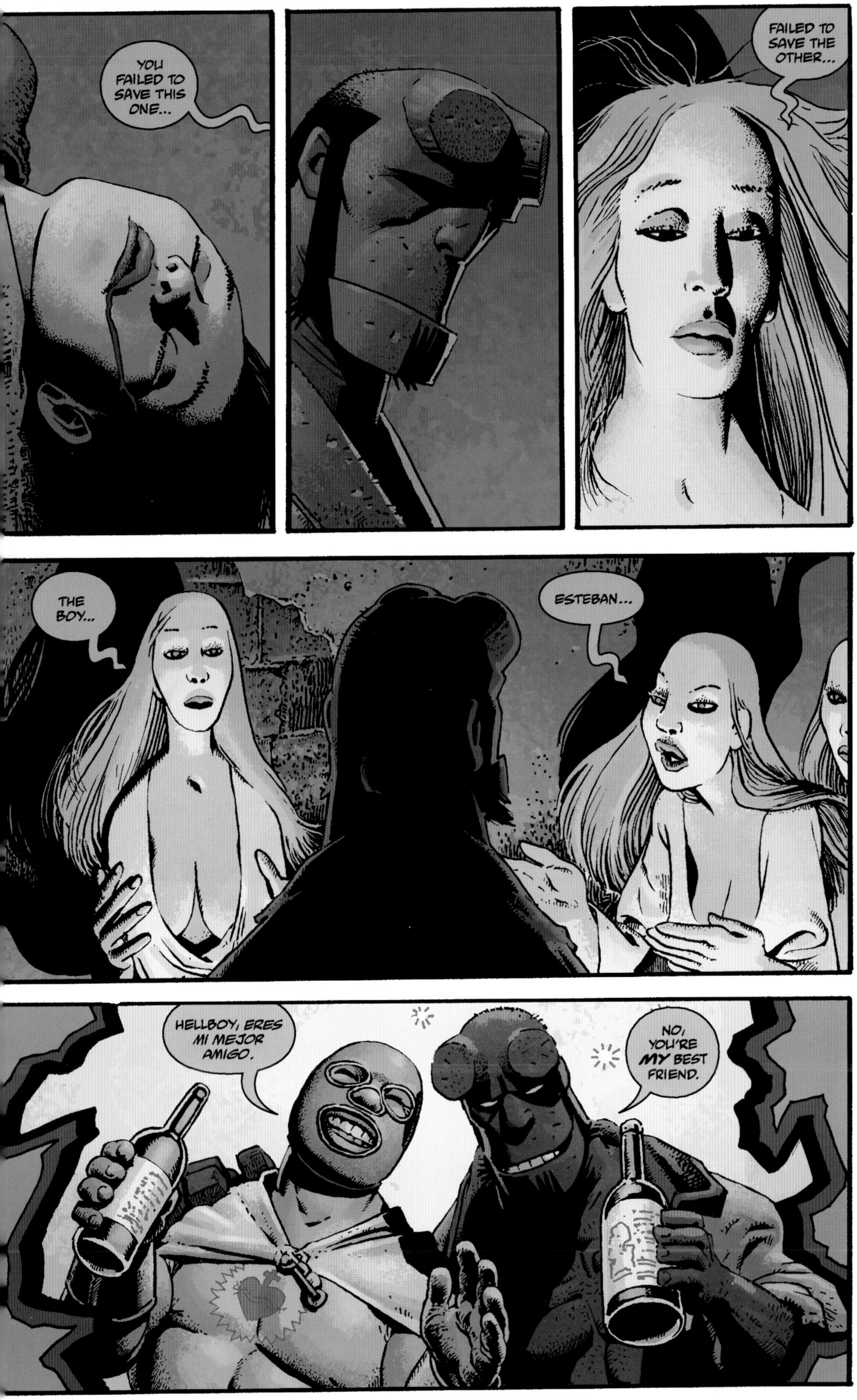
YOU FAILED TO SAVE THIS ONE...
FAILED TO SAVE THE OTHER...
THE BOY...
ESTEBAN...
HELLBOY, ERES MI MEJOR AMIGO.
NO, YOU'RE MY BEST FRIEND.

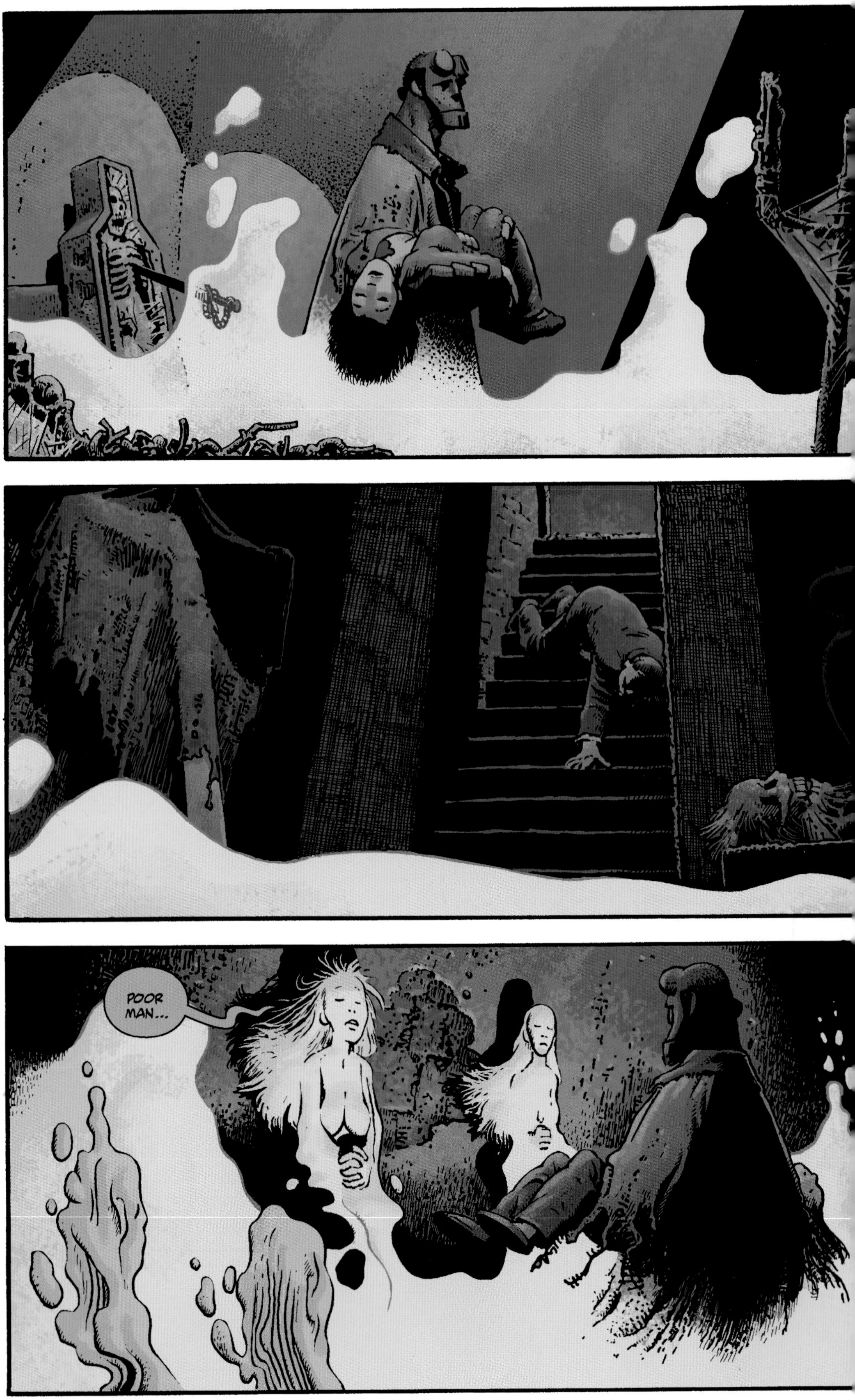
POOR MAN...

SILVER BULLETS...

I MEANT TO USE THEM...TO KILL MYSELF...

BUT I WAS NEVER STRONG ENOUGH.

SONIA...

FORGIVE ME.

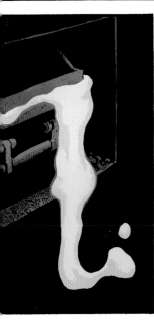

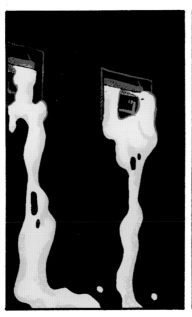

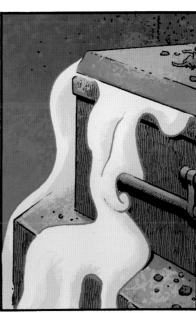

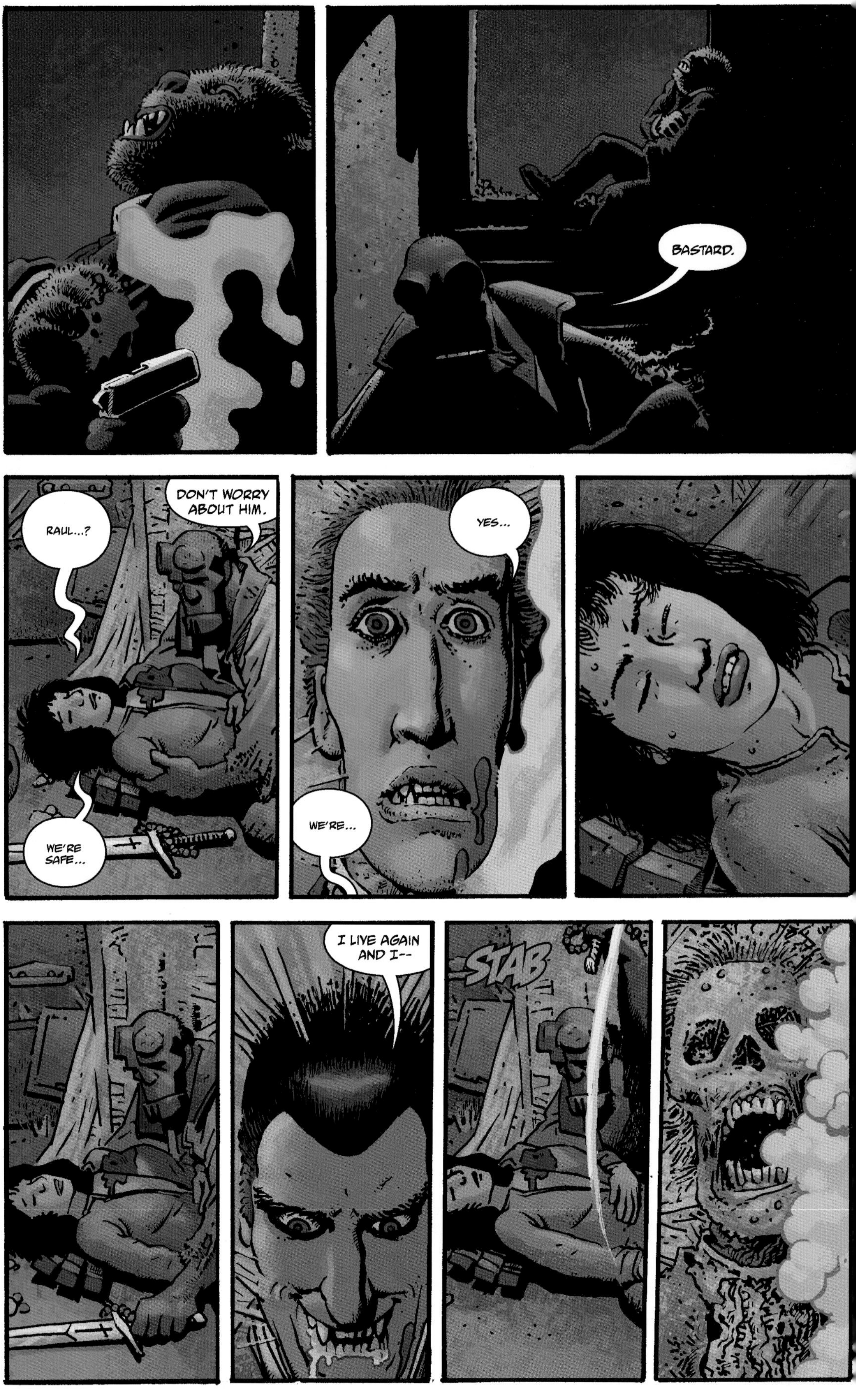
BASTARD.
RAUL...?
DON'T WORRY ABOUT HIM.
WE'RE SAFE...
YES...
WE'RE...
I LIVE AGAIN AND I--
STAB

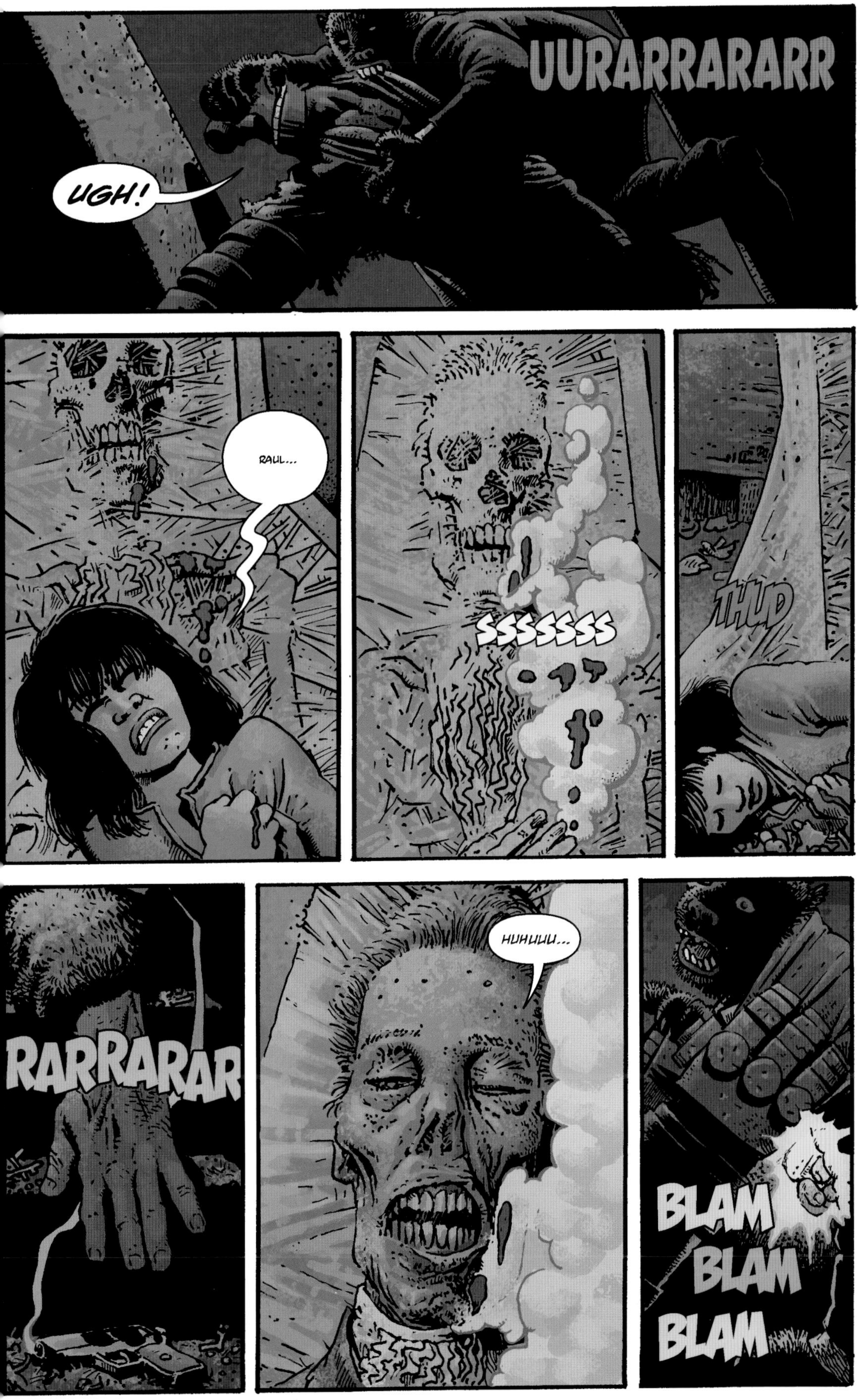
UURARRARARR
UGH!
RAUL...
SSSSSSS
THUD
RARRARAR
HUHUUU...
BLAM
BLAM
BLAM

RAUL, PLEASE...

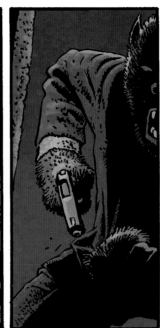

HANG ON, KID.

DON'T.

BLAM

SON OF A--

RAARR!